I Sold my Body
FOR A GOOD PAYCHECK

My Life as a Black Female Coal Miner

By **Janice Davison- Heller**

Chronicles of a Davison

First Edition

Editing by Lorrie Brown
Editing by DeAnna L Carpenter
Editing by LionLike MindState
Cover Design by BlesseD' Signs

Dedications

This book is dedicated to my three children Adrian, Myca, John, and all my grandchildren. I love you with all my heart.   This book is also dedicated to all the hardworking coal miners who have risked their lives to feed their families.

TABLE OF CONTENTS

PREFACE

This book was written through a difficult time in the life of Janice Davison-Heller. Although she almost faced death fearlessly throughout her unprecedented career, the death of a good friend brought her to her knees and then to her pen. Many loved ones encouraged this written venture including but not limited to, her doctor, her daughter, and her aunt Shirley. As you read you will laugh, you may cry and sometimes cringe as you walk through her experience in the coal mines of Indiana and Illinois. Working in the coal mine has typically been a field of work dominated by men, but Janice broke this stereotype by joining a force of little-known coal mining women. Janice discovered what she could accomplish by simply being determined to never quit. She loved her family unconditionally. She overcame abuse, worked through injuries that would have caused many to quit, made lifelong friends and learned a lot about herself along the way. This book was written during a period of grief and was used as a tool to demonstrate to Janice that the tragedy she witnessed at the mine was a signal that it was time to begin a new chapter in her life. This chapter is designed to be a testament for others to share with anyone who cares to listen. This book will take you on a ride through the life of Janice, to share in her triumphs and tragedies as she worked in the coal mines in the seventies. You will have the opportunity to get a sneak peek into the daily life of a coal miner who happens to be a woman. You will understand what drove her to take on one of the hardest and most dangerous jobs that the mine had to offer and learn why even after numerous injuries, she would do it all over again if she could. The following are short stories about different times and incidents that took place in the life and career of one woman of more than 25 years.

INTRODUCTION

M y body should have given up on me a long time ago. Probably right after I broke my back the first time, but still managed to push through the jarring pain against the doctor's orders to report back to work. Call me crazy or hardheaded, or call it determination, grit, resilience, and a little bit of desperation. I was a woman set on making sure her family was well provided for. Despite the bangs and bruises, working at the coal mines ensured that I was able to do just that. Yes, you read that correctly: I am, rather was, a coal miner. A black coal miner. A black female coal miner at that.

So, when I heard about the coal industry and that they were hiring, my curiosity was piqued. I saw an opportunity, something that could be for me and would guarantee that better life I so desperately wanted for me and my son. My grandmother was against it from the start, but I was determined to make a way out of what seemed like no way. Deep down, I wanted to make her proud. I wanted to show her and my family that even though I didn't finish high school, I could still succeed and make a difference. My grandmother provided me with a solid foundation, and it was up to me to build the rest. She made sure that I had a relationship with God and Jesus Christ, which kept me sane, covered and protected in the years that followed.

When I look back at my time in the mines, I often wonder how I managed to do it all. A 2014 study by the NSW Minerals Council reported that only 9 percent of full-time workers in the mining industry were female. This study, the first of its kind, was conducted after I left the mine, so the percentage of female workers at the mines the same time as I was, is likely lower. It was dangerous work, but at the time when I was in it, it didn't seem so dangerous because I was resolute. The independence I felt and experienced because I was a coal miner helped me to feel good about myself and take pride in my untraditional path. I come from a lineage of hard workers; the background of the Davison family is that we have a strong work ethic. I took my job seriously because I knew I was adding to and keeping our family legacy as hard workers alive.

I share intimate moments from my life, specifically the years when I worked in the mines, which spans two decades, and I share a bit on the years after leaving the industry. I hope that through this book, anyone reading it will be encouraged to move forward and to trust that they will make it through to the other side of whatever stands in their way. This book also allows me to give voice to life in the coal mines and shed light on a sector that most people just don't know about. This book is for those brave men and women who risked their lives underground so that the people of this country could have their basic needs met.

Disclaimer/Name Change Warning: To respect the organizations I worked for and the people I worked with, the names of companies and people have been changed.

MY GRANDMOTHER

I was raised by my grandmother, Mary E. Smith-Davison, since I was 6 months old. During my childhood it was just the two of us who lived in the house unless she had renters there. I grew up in a house full of love thinking she was my mother. I never lacked for anything, but as I got older around the age of six, I realized something was missing, my mom and dad.

My grandmother was strict, she was old school, and didn't play no games. I grew up doing chores, cleaning my room, doing the dishes, dusting, mopping and laundry on Saturdays. I dreaded doing the laundry, we used to pull all our dirty clothes down the street in a shiny, bright red wagon, to the laundromat. I was afraid the other neighborhood kids would see me. The laundry mat was a long block away from the house and every time a car would pass by, I would turn my head away. I did this from the first step I took out of the house. After the laundry was done, we would go outside with those big ole shears and trim the bushes. I knew my grandmother was much older than my friend's parents, so I was aware that she depended on my help.

When I started asking my grandmother questions about my parents, she was honest and would tell me that I had a father who was in the military, and He would be back to visit. My dad was her son, so he suggested that I stay with his mother and that's how I ended up living with my grandmother in Vincennes, Indiana. My grandmother was in her late 50's around this time. She explained to me that my mother had two small babies before I was born, and she couldn't take care of me. My grandmother also told me that my parents loved me, but this was the best decision for them to make. I was there as an only child and at times I was lonely. Most of my friends had both parents in the home with a house full of children. My favorite place to visit was at the Goffners' house, to play with Tracy, my best friend. I practically lived there. I could always feel the warmth of the love and good energy at the Goffners' home. It felt like laughter and full bellies. We would eat dinner together as a family. Tracy's parents always made me feel like one of their own kids. It was filling that growing void I was missing from home. Typical normalcy. My grandmother worked as a nanny for a well-known doctor and his family. So sometimes she would be late or even stay for the weekend when they went out of town. On some occasions, my grandmother would take me with her to work. The doctor had three daughters, two of which were girls around my age. The girls had a really cool tree house. I loved climbing up the nailed tree ladder. Daydreaming from the top and pretending all the things little girls play pretend. I had so much fun playing with them. His wife was kind to us, she would give my grandmother the clothes that their girls had outgrown. I would always have something nice to wear to school and at church.

Every Sunday, my grandmother took me to Second Baptist, a small church located around the corner from our home. We would walk there no matter what, whether the sun, the rain or even snowy blistering cold weather. One time my dog Friskie followed us to church, and my grandmother repeatedly told me that the dog needed to go home. I yelled at him and tried to scare him to leave but, this time he wouldn't. This had happened before in the past and I guess this was the day that my grandmother was fed up. The next thing I knew grandma pulled out her switch and smacked little Friskie like he was one of us kids. He ran back so fast all I could see was his tail between his legs. I cried quietly to myself. I knew better to even mumble a word.

Second Baptist was the only black church in my community during that time; almost every black family who lived in the area would be at church, come Sunday morning. I learned how to pray at an early age and was required to attend Sunday School in the morning and service in the afternoon. This is when church felt all day long on occasion. The church congregation consisted mostly of our family. The thing I enjoyed most about our small church was getting to hang out with all my cousins and friends on Sunday.

I was serious about committing my life to God. I made the choice to get baptized when I was 11 years old. Into the water I went and out I came anew. I joined the choir later and even went on church camp trips with other youth groups. On some Sundays, I would hang out with my favorite cousins then go over to my aunt Annie's house where I would eat all the home cooked meals that my stomach could take. Aunt Annie always had a spread of mouthwatering food on the table: Fresh-out-the-oven homemade rolls topped with butter saturated and still running off the sides, dressing, and don't forget the macaroni and cheese with the slightly burnt crust. I remember and I can almost still smell the scent of well-seasoned fried chicken and hot earthy greens that welcomed us as soon as we walked through her front door. The air was moist and thick at aunt Annie's house. The humidity of her humanity and love toward the family was something one could sense. Aunt Annie would "get down and burn" in the kitchen on a Sunday afternoon. Sometimes there would be as many as 15 people there to eat. All you could hear was laughter and joy throughout the house. It was my favorite sound. My aunt Annie and grandmother were both amazing cooks. They came from a small place in Kentucky, and they didn't have too much but they could take a little bit of something and make it taste so good! They each had a reputation amongst family and friends for "putting their foot" in everything they cooked. My grandmother loved cooking and occasionally she would let me come in the kitchen while they worked their magic. When I got older, and started cooking for my own family, I passed the gift along. Now I see my children enjoying cooking for their kids and I know I'm looking at the love passed down from my grandmother and aunt.

On other Sundays at our house, my grandmother would always have fried chicken with fresh green beans, fresh tomatoes, which were grown by her younger brother J.C in his garden, and as always, a delicious dessert. On the table she kept a jar full of cucumbers and onions spiced with vinegar. My grandmother could rival even the most celebrated baker, especially when it came down to those lemon meringue pies, peach cobbler, and my favorite, black berry cobbler. Whenever my father came to visit, she would make him a sweet potato pie. My grandmother also loved canning vegetables. She canned them in the summer, and we would eat them in the winter. Our basement ledge held mason jars filled with tomatoes, juices, green beans, and fresh jelly. As she got older, I would help tighten the lids on the jars as she was losing mobility in her fingers and hands. Grandma always kept fresh corn in the freezer. I never realized how prepared she was. One thing is for certain: We never went hungry in the wintertime.

Grandma was born a hustler and could always find a way to bring money in. She would rent a room to a young college student and on occasion, she would also rent out the basement. Once, a married couple stayed with us. They were seasonal apple pickers from Florida. They would stay a couple of months, leave, then come back during picking season, which was usually in early summer around June and July. I would tag along with them sometimes on Saturdays and I always worked hard. I learned what to look for and how to discern a "Bad Apple". After the day was done, I'd come back home with a pocket full of cash. The red apples brought me green money. I was fortunate that all the house guests respected my grandmother and nothing bad ever happened to us. You never know what anyone is truly capable of.

One time, two sisters who were from Gary, were attending Vincennes University, rented a room from grandma. A few months into staying with us, they ran up the telephone bill. My grandmother called their dad to collect the money. Their father made a special four-hour drive to the house and paid the bill. He also gave them a beat down and they never touched the phone again, not even to make a local call. The girls stayed with us for a year and moved on.

My grandmother's only daughter aunt Shirley lived in California, and she was my favorite aunt. I got to know her well because she spent a lot of time at the house when she lived in Indiana. The best part of her visit was her bringing my favorite cousin's home, the twins Ann and Tony, Kim, Kathy, Lisa, and Lynnie. And later came baby Alex. My cousins and I were a tight crew, we rolled deep and we were always getting into something. The craziest memory I have is one when I was with the Twins. We were walking to Esters Mart to buy some candy. One of us dared each other to run across the street with our eyes closed. Only one of us was brave enough to do it. All I remember was someone yelling, "Ready, Set, Go". The next thing I knew, one of the twins was screaming and yelling while laid out in the street! A car had run her over as she attempted to cross the street. The ambulance had to come. We had to wait. We had to pray. By the grace of God, it was a minor accident. We had a babysitter named "Mabel" who was supposed to be watching us, instead she was busy with the younger kids when we snuck away. We knew Mabel liked to drink and when she was with us, she never kept an eye on us. My aunt and grandmother were furious with her. Later, that evening I thought I was in trouble because I was the oldest of the kids, but they were just glad my cousin was ok. Poor Mabel lost her job that day.

MY BIRTH PARENTS

My father Sylvester Davison Jr, was a Master Sergeant (MSgt) in the Air Force. He served and survived both the Korean and Vietnam Wars and retired after completing 20 years. I rarely saw him when I was a child. I remember receiving packages from him around my birthday and sometimes at Christmas. When I was around six years old, my father came to visit. My dad was a handsome man. He would always dress nicely, with slacks, a buttoned shirt, polished shoes, and a slick hat. He smelled so good. He enjoyed wearing nice cologne. He had a Cadillac, which he drove to Indiana from California. My father had seven children besides me, and I was his oldest. My dad had remarried by the time he came to visit, so he brought his wife and their kids. They came and stayed with us for a week. My father had purchased my grandmother's beautiful and spacious three-bedroom home that we lived in. She loved our house. He made sure everything was fixed and repaired while he was there. I remember being shy and standoffish around my dad. I barely knew him.

Before he left one of the girls pulled out the string on my Chatty Kathy doll. I was so upset. My dad and his wife took the doll to a doll hospital and got her fixed. I was happy that he cared. My dad was living in Sacramento, California. He had to get back to the Los Rios School District where he was working as an on-campus Police Sergeant.   I understood that he was busy traveling and working.

When I met my mother, Theda Brown, I was around 12 years old when she came to take me back to Omaha NE. My mother was short and petite with big brown eyes. She had thick shoulder length hair. Her face was beautiful, speckled with freckles.

 My mother had eight children, four girls and four boys. They all came down on the Greyhound bus to visit Indiana. When my grandmother first told me she was coming, I felt excited. I couldn't wait to get to know my mother, my brothers, and sisters. When they arrived, I took my siblings through the neighborhood introducing them to everybody. I was proud to show off my family. My mom was staying at grandma's for a week. At first, everything was new, fun, and exciting but that wore off fast. My siblings and I were playing in the basement, and we got into a huge argument about me carrying the "Davison" last name instead of "Brown". I knew then that I was staying in Indiana. I was a small-town girl. I wasn't ready for the big city.

My Mother was quiet, with a gentle spirit but she didn't comfort me, nor did she talk to me much. She mostly spoke with my grandmother making plans. When it was time for us to leave, I ran and hid under the big dining room table. The table was covered with an ornate tablecloth that almost touched the ground. I thought she couldn't see me. They could both see me, most likely. I would hide there often whenever I needed some me time. A kiddie place it was my safe space. My stress shelter or shelter from stress. After the door closed, my grandmother told me to come out. She knew where I was the entire time. She sat me down and explained to me that her and my mother thought it was best for me to remain in Indiana. They left and I never said goodbye. I didn't see them again until I was 16, when I traveled to Omaha to visit, this time I was the one on the Greyhound. The trip was over 15 hours long with all the connection routes and strangers. I was scared, I had never been on a trip that long before. I went there in the summertime and stayed for a month. I was happy to see my mom and my family. I met so many aunties, uncles, cousins, and grandparents. Every time we left the house, I was meeting a new family member. Everyone was kind and welcoming. My mother was working a lot. She worked full-time for a well-known cereal company. My brothers were "running" the streets, so I hung out with my sisters. We spent a lot of time at my mom's dad's house. My grandfather was a handsome man full of character, he liked to entertain, tell jokes and was a lot of fun. The house was full of family running in and out. At my mom's mother's house, it was different, it was quiet, clean and nobody was running in and out. My grandmother was a beautiful woman, she had a nice petite shape with long grey hair. She was quiet like my mother. They were women of few words. My brother Bruce was living there. Bruce and I were the only ones who had the same mom and dad. My other siblings had a different father than us. Omaha was a lot to take in, coming from a small town. I was ready to get back to Indiana after that trip.

IT TAKES A VILLAGE

My first-born child, Adrian, was the most beautiful baby I had ever seen. When the nurses first placed him in my arms, I thought they brought me the wrong baby. There was only one other woman who gave birth that night and she had a girl. So, believe it or not, he was mine. Adrian was just so gorgeous. He had a head full of wavy, jet-black hair and deep, almond-shaped, curious eyes. As I held him, with his tiny finger wrapped around mine, I knew that I would do whatever it took to provide for him. And that smile? My goodness, that smile melted away the insecurity I felt around being a teenage mother.

My pregnancy was met with disappointment, and I felt shunned by some of my family and friends. I was 17 years old, and I didn't have a clue on how to raise a baby. To add to everything, the father of my son wanted nothing to do with him or me. I was the only one in my crew who had gotten pregnant at such a young age. I was scared and nervous. I stayed at Tracy's house a lot during that time, her parents were my support system during my pregnancy and helped me feel right at home the entire time. Her mom hosted a baby shower for me and the only people that came were from her family. None of my friends and family showed up. I was so embarrassed. I remember realizing in that moment how my friends and family felt about me being pregnant. They didn't agree with it or support it, and they showed this very clearly through their actions. I woke up that day to a harsh truth: My pregnancy wasn't accepted. I was young and had sex prematurely, which resulted in me being pregnant. It was an innocent mistake, yet they didn't see it that way. Thankfully, my grandmother, my best friend, my play mother as I called my best friend's mother, and her father saw me for me. They didn't judge me. They opened their arms and doors to me. They celebrated with me. I was so blessed to have them because I didn't have to sit in my pity, pain, and shame. And when Adrian was born, they treated him just like their grandson.

With that ear-to-ear smile and a laugh that could melt any heart, Adrian was joy personified. He never had a problem with anyone holding him. I started to notice in his first few weeks that he slept a lot during the day and at night, which was unusual for newborns. He slept so much that I would wake him up to ensure he wouldn't die of sudden infant death syndrome (S.I.D.S). It wasn't until he was around two months old that I noticed he had respiratory issues. One evening my grandmother advised me that A.D., as we called him, was short of breath. I took him to the hospital recommended pediatrician who I didn't know very well. After two hours of waiting in a busy lobby, he checked his chest and kept us for about 20 minutes and sent us home with cough medicine. I trusted his recommendation and left. I went home only to get a scolding from my grandmother. She told me that he had more than a cold and she made me call my OBGYN. We rushed back out the door. Once my OBGYN checked A. D's chest, he advised us to go to the ER immediately. That's when I found out my baby boy had a breathing issue. That night they placed him in an oxygen tent, a plastic tube that zipped over his whole body. I had never seen anything like that before. I cried and couldn't help but think that my baby was going to have long-term side effects. We went through this for several years. He would be Ok and then out of the blue he would have trouble breathing. He would make noises as if he couldn't catch his breath.

I experienced quite a few scares with my son and his health, but nothing compares to this one time when my aunt Shirley had come to visit. I was in my bedroom when I noticed that A.D's skin had turned blue. I yelled for my aunt, who was a nurse, to help. She quickly rushed over and turned him upside down, held him by the feet, and patted him on the back. By God's grace, he slowly started breathing again. I was so grateful for her wisdom and knowledge that saved my sons life.

I DIDN'T HAVE A CLUE

I dropped out of high school months before giving birth to my son. I replaced going to school with working two jobs. The desperation of parenthood prescribed that I needed to be able to provide for him, so I took whatever job was available. Which meant at that time, working at a local nursing home and the town's café. The two jobs couldn't have been any more different. The epitome of night and day. I worked the graveyard shift at the café five days a week from 3 a.m. to 10 a.m. Then, I would walk home, change clothes, feed A.D., and walk to the nursing home to work a second swing shift six days a week from 2 p.m. to 9 p.m. This effectively gave me a total of just over two days off per week from both jobs. Although it was a lot of work, the hours worked out, but I had little time to rest before going from one job to the next. Even with both gigs, I still struggled to make ends meet. At that time, minimum wage was a bare minimum. With both jobs combined, I earned $6 an hour. Close to nothing, but I managed to make it work to keep us afloat; and honestly, that was the only thing that mattered to me.

The nursing home was small and easy to get around, my first day was rough. The lead nurse took me on a tour of the floor and introduced me to patients. As we stepped into one room, an older man in his 70s shouted in both a scared and stonewalled tone, "Get that nigger out of here; I don't want her to touch me." The nurse scolded him and told him that he couldn't speak to me that way. Shocked but mostly appalled, I kept calm. After we left the room, I was so mad that I didn't want to go back. And when I thought the day couldn't get any more eventful, it did. About two hours later, the nurse that I was assisting asked me to take over and feed this frail little lady. The nurse handed me a turkey baster and dipped it into a bowl that had a brownish liquid mush in it. It looked like oats. I began to feed her. A few minutes into feeding her, she started choking and moaning at the same time. I didn't stop because the nurse told me the patient was ok. The head nurse walked by and heard the lady then shouted, "What are you doing?!? That's a death rattle! Take that out of her mouth." I dropped the baster immediately, stepping back and was terrified all over again. The woman died within five minutes of me attempting to feed her. The head nurse was upset with my assisting nurse for entrusting me to feed the older woman while ignoring her moaning. I didn't know any different or better. I had lost my first patient and she died while I was feeding her. All I could think about at that moment was the paperwork I completed during my training. There was a line that stated, "If a patient died, I would be responsible to clean them up. Luckily, since it was my first day, they let me leave. When I went to bed that evening, all I could think about was how the little old lady's eyes followed me everywhere I went in that room. Her eyes were open when she passed, and I felt her eyes on me. I was totally creeped out. The eyes don't just close like they do in the movies when you close them, they open right back up! That night, I closed my eyes and saw her eyes still open.

The next day when I walked through the door, the head nurse looked surprised when she saw me. Her wide eyes flashed, and her grin gave a half smile. She didn't expect me to be back to work so soon. She just didn't know how determined I was. Even death, although it shook me up for a moment, would not prevent me from doing what I had to do for myself and my son. I'm sure she thought I was going to quit considering the crazy first day I had, but I didn't. I came back and kept coming back. During my time at the nursing home, I cared for 25 patients. One of whom was that very same grumpy old man who called me a nigger on my first day. After caring for him for a while, he began to soften around me, and I built trust and a rapport with him. We became friends and it got to the point that I was the only person he wanted to take care of him. He often gave all the other aides and nurses a hard time but would instantly calm down as soon as I entered his room. Over time, I realized that some of the people in the nursing home, like this older gentleman, didn't get any visitors. So, when they gave us a hard time, it was their way of acting out and expressing their loneliness. Then, we had the aides and nurses who were working long shifts, who were burnt out and only there to collect a paycheck. One time, I came back from my day off to find one of my bed-ridden patients with a handprint on her cheek. Her face was swollen and red. She couldn't speak, she would just moan. When I went to lunch that afternoon, I told a coworker that her face was swollen, that's when she told me that a seasoned aide had smacked her. Apparently, the aide was feeding her, and the woman spit up her food and it landed on the aide's uniform. The aide had the nerve to talk about it that same day with other coworkers. I was furious because everyone including management knew who hit her and she was never disciplined. The nursing home was full of young kids who called out a lot. The work was hard, so they barely had a reliable staff. This was my first lesson about compassion.

I got emotionally attached really quickly to my patients, they had me going to the store bringing back snacks and coffee. I heard all the stories about their families and who they were before they came to the nursing home.

Harley's Café was a much-needed change of scenery and helped me to balance out the emotional nature of working at the nursing home. During my shifts, I was able to give my mind a break from the life and death cycle and simply focus on something I loved: Food. I enjoyed baking and having time alone. I spent most of my time at Harley's baking in the basement of the restaurant. The Café was a family friendly business. Harley the owner, was a workaholic who ran his restaurant with the help of his two sons. I worked with his youngest son, Joe, the café butcher, from time to time. He was a young man eager to please his father but to no avail. Harley's wife had passed, and he turned from a workaholic into an alcoholic. Harley often took his anger and frustrations out on Joe. Joe and I would be down in the basement preparing the food and minding our business when his father would come downstairs, causing an explosive scene. He always went over to his son cussing and fussing, being loud and irate, and I feared that he would eventually direct his anger at me. Thankfully he never did. Joe would leave for weeks at a time, returning only when his father had calmed down.

Despite his volcanic temperament, I learned a lot from Harley, and I loved this job. Harley was very intentional about the food he served and made sure he had enough help to meet and exceed his desire for quality food and service. He hired only older woman to fry the chicken and he used real potatoes to fry and mash. I would watch the ladies peel hundreds of potatoes. Sometimes, there would be one person peeling potatoes for her entire shift. The food tasted good. It was fresh, seasoned well, and tasted like black folks had prepared it. There were no black folk in the kitchen though. I was the only black person who worked at Harley's at that time. All the staff, and even Harley himself, were white. The food at Harley's was so good and had such a reputation that people would drive from other counties and small towns to eat there.

Working two jobs as an 18-year-old taught me how to grow up fast and gave me valuable life lessons that I still use today. At the nursing home, I learned how to be empathic and how to care for people. I learned to treat my patients, and anyone I worked with or encountered, as I would want to be treated. At Harley's, I enhanced my cooking skills and became quite adept at making noodles from scratch. And thanks to my time at Harley's, I know how to make a mean peach cobbler and all kinds of pies, including lemon meringue.

Before these two jobs, I worked as a line cook, I worked at two different factories, I worked seasonally raking leaves in the fall, shoveling snow in the winter, detasseling corn in the summer and even babysitting from time to time.

I finally managed to save enough money to buy a car which cost $500. A family friend was selling their blue Oldsmobile and allowed me to make monthly payments. I was ecstatic and so was Grandma. The car wasn't much to look at, but it ran well. We could finally get rid of the lil red wagon. I could finally show my face; I was in the car passing by.

.

THE DATE

Friday nights were for dancing. They brought a much-needed respite from my intense work schedule. My girls and I would go out to meet people, dance and simply have a good time. When I danced, I was able to breathe. Everything that I was carrying or stressing about evaporated while on that dance floor. I felt light and carefree. It felt good to not have to worry, and to put my responsibilities on hold albeit only for a few hours while I immersed myself in the rhythms of the sounds cranking from the DJs turntable.

We went to a small local bar that played mostly disco music. Within minutes of being at that spot, a beautiful man asked me to dance. He was lean, about six feet tall, with beautiful hazel eyes. We danced and talked all night. He was from a small town called Lawrenceville, in Illinois, about 15 minutes from where I lived. He asked me out on a date and the following Saturday, he picked me up. He wanted to make me dinner at his house but, first he wanted to stop by his mom's home nearby. We talked on the long drive through the boonies. During one of our conversations, I complained to him about how some of the white people were mean to me at the nursing home and the racism I experienced. I discovered that we shared similar experiences. He told me had a daughter, but he and her mother were no longer together. His daughter stayed with him on the weekends. Once we arrived at his family's house, I was embarrassed to find out that his mother was white. That was my first real lesson on keeping my mouth shut. He didn't seem to mind because we were connecting, but I felt horrible inside. After leaving his family's home, we drove about 5 miles up the road to his house where he made us dinner. As soon as we pulled into his yard, I saw a deer gutted open, hanging from a tree. I knew right away that he was a country boy who liked to hunt. He had a nice spot, a two-bedroom trailer that he kept clean and tidy. The food was good, and our conversation was easy and light. As the night went on, he began telling me about his job.

"I work at the coal mine," he said, bragging a bit.

Everyone knew that men who worked for the coal mine had money and benefits. I was excited to hear that he worked for a coal mine. I was so curious about his job, so I listened intently. "You can make a lot of money in the mines," he continued. I kept wondering if there could be a job opportunity for me, even though I was a woman.

"Oh really?" I pushed him on. I continued to bombard him with questions one after the other.

"What about women?" I blurted out. He looked at me puzzled.

"What about women?" he asked.

"Well, I remember someone telling me that women were not allowed to work in the mines..."

"Ha, I don't know who told you that," he scoffed in a playful manner.

"Well, my uncle works in a mine in Kentucky, and I have never heard him talk about women in his mine."

"I work for Illinois Coal Mine, in Queensburg not Kentucky...", he replied, with a hint of sarcasm in his voice.

"Do women work at your mine?" I asked.

"We have several women working at my mine. You should go there and put in an application. You sound interested" he said with amusement. It all sounded too good to be true.

I obviously must have had an excited look on my face to prompt such a reaction from him. I think he could tell that I was more interested in learning about the coal mine than in dating him. We only saw each other once after that, we met up and went out dancing. He was nice and good looking, but I really wanted to *work* with him instead of dating him.

AN APPLICATION TO REMEMBER

T he idea that I could get paid as much as a man was thrilling. The amount of money I could make in one job was what I was struggling to make at the two jobs I had combined. I told my four girlfriends from school about applying at the mine, since they all were out of work. At the time, it seemed as if there weren't enough well-paid jobs in our town to go around and the coal mine seemed like the solution to the shortage. Out of my girlfriends, I could only convince two of them to come apply. These two girls were sisters who came from a large family.

The next day the three of us hopped in my car, drove an hour to the employment office, filled out the new hire paperwork and awaited our fate. To our surprise, they sent us over to the coal mine that day and the admin gave us authorization to speak with the lead at the Illinois Coal Mine. "Here is your paperwork. Go to portal two and look for Tim." At portal two there were about thirty steep steps that ran alongside a grassy hill, which led to a site where the offices were. It was difficult to tell that there was a coal mine since it was underground. When we spoke with Tim, he confirmed that they were hiring and asked us to give him a couple of weeks to get back with us. None of us thought he would call us back, so we went back to our usual routines.

During my time at the nursing home, I worked with some of the laziest people I have ever met, which made me realize that not everyone was cut out for this type of work. There were mostly young people working there only for the paycheck and it showed in how they treated the patients. They lacked empathy and compassion, two qualities that are necessary when working with seniors in an assisted living facility. And since the nursing home was often understaffed, a lot of this behavior was seldom reprimanded because they needed people to work. I think people forget that they will get old eventually and at some point, they may need someone to take care of them, too. It's almost as if some of those aides had never heard the simple yet powerful proverb, the Golden Rule: "Do unto others as you would have others do unto you." Luke 6:31.

One day while feeding a patient, the secretary came in and said, "You got a phone call," she said. At first, I was scared because I only got calls if something was wrong with my son Adrian. "Hello?" I said when I picked up the phone.

"Is this Janice?" A male voice asked.

"Yes," I answered hesitantly.

"This is Tim from the mine. It has been difficult getting a hold of you..." he said.

I held my breath.

"I would like to make you an offer to work for the Illinois Coal Mine," he said hesitantly. This call was good news!

"Yes, I accept." I said promptly, exhaling with a smile. I had just accepted the position without the slightest idea what I was getting myself into. Tim kept the call short. He gave me the time, date, and location for the hiring orientation on that following Monday.

"Thank you!" I said, screaming on the inside.

According to Tim, he had called my house and spoken with my grandmother days prior and shared with her who he was and that he wanted to offer me a job at the coal mine. My grandmother had curtly replied that no daughter of hers would work at the coal mine and she abruptly hung up on him. He called me at the nursing home because he suspected that she would not pass the message on to me. He could have easily moved on to another applicant and by that time, I had almost forgotten about the mine job application, but I am glad he didn't. He had no idea how much that call meant to me. They only called two of us back, out of the sisters only one really wanted to work there, and she was not offered the position. I was excited thinking my girlfriend and I would be driving and working together, but she later declined the position.

Later that evening, my grandmother never even bothered to mention anything to me about receiving a call from the mine. I was so grateful that Tim called me at my job. It was obvious that my grandmother did not want me to work there, we never spoke about it. When I told her I got the job, she just rolled her eyes and walked away. When she was a young girl, she lived in Kentucky and her school took a field trip to a local mine and she remembered getting into a small cage and riding down underground. The field trip scared her so much she decided right then and there, that was the most dangerous job ever. I believe in my heart she thought I was going to get myself killed.

NEW JOB AT THE MINE

I t was in September 1979 when I first started at the mine, I was 23 years old. After a week of training and orientation, I was ready to see and experience the mine with my own eyes. The training took place in a large room, and we learned things like CPR, mine safety, air quality testing, the importance of tubed oxygen which was pumped in by industrial fans, how to find good locations in the mine to breath during an emergency, how to locate where the phones are to call above, how to find a safe way above if the power was knocked out and what the evacuation strategy was. They gave us four complete classes that we got certifications for.

That Friday couldn't have come soon enough. It was the day we were to go underground. Our class had 12 miners and four of them were women. We were told to purchase a lunch pail, steel toe boots, a coal mining belt, and work gloves. The mine officials provided us with safety glasses, a hard hat with a lamp light. I purchased my miner's belt for $15 from a guy who worked at the mine.

I wore long johns underneath my clothes, a pair of old jeans, a tee-shirt, and my new steel toe boots. Nervousness and excitement consumed every inch of my body as our class walked up the ramp to the elevator. I couldn't believe we were finally headed underground. The elevator was small but still large enough to carry the entire class. As we stepped inside, the gate closed slowly behind us and our descent into the Earth began. The ride seemed so long and indeed it was, especially since we were using an elevator. It took us five minutes to get to the bottom, which was 800 feet below the surface. The air was thin, and it only got thinner the more we descended. We stepped off the elevator and we were met with darkness after we passed through the last set of doors. A musty smell immediately filled my nostrils, and I had a taste of dirt in my mouth. I remember my mouth feeling dry and suddenly, I was thirsty. I had to take slow, deep breaths through my nose. This was the first time I had ever been underground.

Being underground was a whole world in itself. Although I had spent some time in a cave in Tennessee once, nothing compared to what I was seeing before me. A conveyor belt stretched overhead, carrying the coal from one end of the mine to the next. As we inched closer to the belt, the mine manager showed us important safety features, including how to disconnect the power on the belt in case of an emergency. After viewing the conveyor belt, we walked over to the maintenance area where two mechanics met with us. These two men played a very important role. They inspected all the machinery and kept them running. Most importantly, they kept the mine going. After surveying the different machines and gadgets, we moved towards the work unit. To get there, we had to ride in a man trip. A man trip was like a shuttle, or a tram used at amusement parks to transport park attendees. The difference was that the man trip transported coal miners. We saw a total of seven men working. Two men were in buggies, two men were mining, and there were two roof bolters. There was always a mechanic in each unit. Once the workers noticed we were there they shut off the machines and said hello. They were friendly and seemed to like their jobs.

I knew while interacting with and observing the seven men in the work unit that I belonged. I felt at that moment that this job was something that I could truly be proud of. Not only would I be bringing in more money to support myself, but I would be part of a union family as well. I felt deep in my heart that life for me wouldn't be the same. We remained underground for two hours, which allowed us time to get familiar with the area and its inner workings. I was so eager to start, and I couldn't wait for my first full week of work to begin. I noticed right away that not everyone felt the same. Once we returned above ground, several people looked spooked. Their eyes were wide open and full of fear. One guy asked if anyone wanted to buy his lunch bucket or belt. He said that he was not going back down there. One of the women laughed and said that she wasn't going back either.

It took me about sixty minutes to get home from the mine. I smiled each minute, the entire way. I was just so excited and felt bubbly like a glass of champagne. Things were beginning to look up for me and I was ready for the new adventure and the challenge. I wasn't afraid of going underground. I was intrigued by it and wanted to learn more. I wanted to do my best and I was committed to doing and giving just that. Once I got home, I tried to restrain my excitement as best as I could. My grandmother wasn't thrilled about me working at the mines and she didn't ask me how my day or orientation went. She didn't understand my choice to work there, but I knew a better way, a better life awaited me in those mines. I was ready to show her and anyone who may have doubted me that I could do it and I would make it. Trying to sleep that night was hard. I had all the excitement of a child waiting to open gifts on Christmas day.

WHEN THE LIGHTS GO OUT

It didn't take long for me to discover how much of a pain my boss was. He was micromanaging us, hovering over us like a dark cloud that wouldn't let up. Hardly anyone got along with him and that included upper management. He just didn't know how to treat people. But this didn't stop the upper execs from putting him in charge of our cohort. That first week was a very long week for us new hires. Nothing we did was enough to satisfy his demands. We received feedback and praise from other managers, but not from the one assigned to us. He wouldn't even give us a restroom break or allow us to drink water until lunchtime, which was around noon and only for 30 minutes. He was working us like dogs and getting a lot accomplished.

I learned from the seasoned miners that we were allowed a water and restroom break, and it did not have to be at lunchtime. We were so new and green, and we did not know any better. Our boss was so mad at us when we started disappearing for our unannounced breaks. The older miners informed us that he was a bit of a tyrant with everyone. We also learned that he had been fired from a managerial position over at another mine. He was trying to make a name for himself at Illinois Coal and his goal was to move up the ladder as quickly as possible. I guess he thought that being a jerk would show the leadership team that he could keep us all in line. Thankfully, we only worked under him for two weeks before our group was split up and assigned to temporary units.

One of my first jobs was as a general laborer, which included working on the belt head. It was the lowest paying job in the mine, and I was determined to make the most money I could. When I was hired on, I was told that after I worked for six months I could bid to be promoted to another position. This was one of my least favorite jobs in the mine, mainly because it was one of the loneliest jobs. It is just you and hours of darkness and there is no one to watch your back or ensure your safety before, during, or after your shift.

The tunnel was dark, the ceiling was very low, and sometimes, the walls would buckle. The belt head person was required to shovel coal, rocks, and other debris while a large belt ran quickly down the middle with jagged coal on it. Above the belt was timber or metal planks that held the jagged rocks from coming down. If a miner was assigned to the belt head, they would create a makeshift chair with cushions and a table out of wood for the entire eight-hour shift to sit. The examiners would come around once per shift to check the belt and make sure the top was not falling in. They also checked that the air was clear of methane. Besides being boring, the belt head was also one of the most tedious jobs. Not only did you have to watch the belt, but you also were required to shovel the coal 500 feet one way and 500 feet in the opposite direction to ensure the belt head stayed clean. Many times, 500 feet on one end was already cleared because someone from the previous shift had already done it. We had three shifts a day, and each of us had to maintain the belt. During each shift there was almost always a spill of coal that needed to be cleaned up. If there wasn't a spill from the belt, there would be a mess from a side rib or from the top falling in. Anything could happen at any time. It was so important to be able to see where you were going and always have a well charged battery for your lamp.

One evening the mine manager assigned me to the belt head for the night. I got up and walked down the side of the belt to see how far the other person from the previous shift had shoveled. I wanted to be sure I started where they left off, but I needed a hard hat with a fully charged lamp for visibility. The lamp men were responsible for changing the batteries on all the hard hats. When we came up on top, we would have to put our lights back on a charger. That way, they would be ready when we arrived for our next shift. Sometimes, even after being charged, the light would go out without any warning, at which point they would need to be replaced. This was always peculiar because there was no way to gauge how much battery juice was left unless the light went dim. I found a shovel to start cleaning under the belt and then I noticed that the light on my hard hat was starting to go dim. I stopped shoveling right away, went back to my belt head and was fortunate to reach the phone right before my light went completely out. Once the light goes out, you can't get it back on. You can't see the belt, your feet or anything else. It is completely pitch black. And that is dangerous. I was able to get a call through up top to let them know that my light had gone out and requested another light. It was early in my shift and there was still a lot of work left to be done. Once the boss came down to assist me, he realized that I had a bad battery and replaced it. On another occasion, my light went out while I was on clean-up detail. I was by myself with no one around and no phone nearby. I was surrounded by darkness. I just sat down right where I was. I did not want to hurt myself, so I waited until an examiner came by. When he finally arrived, he realized that he needed to call the situation in, so he told me to sit tight and that he would be back with a light for me. I waited for what seemed like an eternity, in the dark, every little sound creeps you out. Each time I heard something fall, I would tense up and wonder what I was doing down there. I asked myself this question several times while I waited. The examiner had completely forgotten that I was down there, waiting for a new light. Everyone had gone back up to the surface at the end of their shift and left for home. I later found out that when my co-workers could not find me at the pick-up point, they assumed I had gotten a ride from another crew. They had no idea that I was still down below, all alone waiting patiently. I remained in the same spot until the next shift arrived two hours later. That was one of the longest nights. I was tired with nothing but my thoughts and cold, hard coal. At that moment, I remembered some miners telling an old miner's tale that if your light went out, it meant your spouse or lover was having an affair. I always laughed about that. Unfortunately, I eventually discovered this old tale to be true. It only took me 6 months to know that this wasn't the job for me. I was told roof bolters, mine operators and mechanics made the most money. So, I decided to bid on the third shift Roof Bolting position. As the first black woman to bid for a roof bolting job at our mine, I was constantly told that I couldn't do it. The roof bolting position, which involves the use of a roof bolter rig to install rock bolts in mines to secure the mine roof, was the only job I wanted. Yes, it was dangerous and not too many women held this position, but I wanted it and knew deep down that I could do it. My requests and bids to be a roof bolter were denied time after time, and I was continually assigned to the belt head. Whenever I was given the opportunity to work on a Roof Bolter for a night, I would beg my mine manager to let me help in units that were shorthanded so I could learn how to use the Roof Bolter. I wanted them to see that I could perform any job at the mine, and with time, maybe they would grant me my request to work as a Roof Bolter. This position would require that I stay busy and active on my feet the whole shift, which would reduce the chances of me falling asleep on the job, a problem that I struggled with a lot.

CAN I GET AN AMEN

A s a general laborer, my work was simple, and I got it done quickly and on time. For the remainder of my shift, I would sit at my post until it was time to go home. Of course, this was quite boring and very mundane, and it became increasingly difficult to stay awake during the entire shift since I did not get enough sleep at home, I was even more exhausted at work. The last thing I needed was to fall asleep on the belt head and die, leaving my child motherless. I know this sounds extreme, but it was a thought that many of us had while working the third shift because it was such a daunting shift to work because it was late at night. One time I dozed off and about a minute or so later, heard a noise. My body tensed up and remained completely still. My mine manager had come down to check on things and when he found me asleep, he kicked my leg. "Amen," I said, pretending that I was praying. I looked up toward him sheepishly.

"I see that you got your shoveling done," he said, choosing to accept my charade. I was glad he did not seem to know that I was up there half asleep, and if he did, he was gracious enough to give me a pass. I heard that he had sent people home for dozing off during their shift. The mine had a zero-tolerance policy regarding sleeping while on the job, and violation of this policy meant immediate termination. "Yes, I always do," I said with a smile. "So, when will I be getting on a unit?" I asked him, changing the subject.

"Be patient, Tweety Bird, I am working on it," he replied. Tweety Bird is a nickname that followed me from high school into the mine. They called me "Tweety Bird", because I have big ole bright eyes with skinny legs and a slim yellow complexion. I was trying to stay on my manager's good side so that I could get on a unit and falling asleep would not help my case at all. Thank God my boss was being nice that night. I think the only reason he did not give me a hard time was because I had completed my job. I wanted to be on an assigned unit very badly, for a full year I was working on different units each night. If someone called out, I was sent there to do their work, until they returned. This was difficult because I never had the opportunity to build a relationship with a crew and my work changed each night. Most of the work was tedious and required me to do a lot of cleaning. I was new and I had to prove I deserved to be in a unit.

On one night, about a month later, I saw a mouse run by my boot. He was relatively small, but I could keep my eyes on him, or so I thought, until I dozed off yet again, only to be woken up by what felt like something crawling inside my shirt and on my chest. I jumped up and started patting my shirt and moving it up and down frantically so he would get out, finally after a few seconds of me jumping all over the place, he ran out of my sleeve. At that point, I was convinced more than ever, that it was time for me to move on from that position.

When a roof bolter position finally opened up, I placed a bid on it, and it was assigned to me. By then, I had acquired enough experience to work on a unit. My new position on the unit did my world a lot of good and gave me the opportunity to work with the same team every day, in the same work area, doing one job. Even my attitude towards work made a 180-degree turn. I was excited by the challenge of learning a new job.

THE SECOND JOB

T he one flaw in working for the mines, is that there was always a strike. I had only been there for a year, and we went on strike for everything, including things like poor work conditions, low hourly pay, mosquito infestation underground, and lack of hot showers. We went on strike so much that I could barely afford to pay my bills. Times were tight and my finances were tighter, so I picked up a second job as a caretaker. I could barely catch a break. My shift at the mine would end at 9 a.m and I'd head right over to the house of an elderly man that I cared for from 10 a.m. to 5 p.m. He had traveling cancer that quickly took a toll on his body. When I first met him, he was able to feed himself and walk. Barely two weeks later, he went blind and eventually stopped eating. Seeing him quickly deteriorate right before my eyes was devastating and hard to witness. His family knew he was dying and together, we did the best we could to ensure his last days were as comfortable as possible.

After about a month of caring for this man, he was hospitalized. When I went to see him, I could barely recognize the man before me. He was not the same person at all. He was on a breathing machine and was in and out of a coma. He was brain dead and the only thing that was keeping him alive was the machine he was hooked up to. His wife and family loved him so much and talked extensively about how much of a great family man he was. My emotions took a big hit seeing him like that and I could only imagine what it was like for his family. I began to reflect on death a lot and thought of my own mortality. After four months of being his caretaker, my client passed away, and at that point, I decided to quit that job.

NEIGHBORLY LOVE

It's funny how childhood friends can become romantic interests later in life. That's the case with Mike, the father of my daughter. Mike and I grew up in a great neighborhood, two houses apart from each other. We never hung out as kids, and it wasn't until much later that anything sparked between us. I was always close to his family. His sisters and I had a great relationship, and I loved his parents. Our families were so close that my son, Adrian, would go over to their house and play with the younger sister Chris. During those days, families were close and looked after each other's children like they were their own. We never worried about our children's safety. We protected one another.

As fate would have it, Mike and I hung out at the same house party in Princeton, about 30 minutes away from our hometown. He asked for a ride home, and that ride home changed everything. We talked and laughed, and I knew then that we both were attracted to one another. After that night, we got into a relationship, and it wasn't long before we got married. We were young, in love and crazy about each other. I had Adrian before I was married to Mike and Mike treated him like his own son. Mike was a good father, and he provided a steady, nurturing, and loving male presence that both my son and I needed at that time. I remember Mike driving me to the coal mine when I was pregnant with our daughter. I was working third shift and I couldn't keep my eyes open long enough to get to work. He would drive me over to the mine and sleep in the car all night until I got off the next day. He never complained about it because I was the only one working at the time. And with time, I gave birth to our beautiful baby girl, named Myca, who looked just like her father.

I was around 25 and even with all the passion and love, we still experienced rough patches in our marriage. We were trying to figure out who we were as individuals while being in a committed union. We both craved independence, respect, and financial stability. Mike ended up securing a job in the Army and was stationed in another state. He wanted us to join him, but I didn't want to give up my job and relocate our family to where he was, which only added fuel to the fire in our marriage. We argued relentlessly during that time. Mike eventually left the Army, a decision he came to on his own, and got a job in Mount Carmel, Illinois, which was where we lived at the time. I think we both had hoped that him leaving the Army and returning to Illinois would turn things around for us, but it didn't. I later discovered that Mike was messing around, and he was seeing other women, which led to even more intense fights and arguments. We divorced shortly after.

Although Mike and I were in a bitter place after the divorce, our families remained close. They helped me raise my daughter, they would call all the time, and often took her to stay with them during the holidays. I was grateful for that level of support, respect, and community. Mike and I weren't destined to be together past the few years that we shared, but this didn't impact the love and bond of our families. To me, this is the true meaning and value of family. Even during great turmoil and duress, they find a way to pull together.

MY PARTNER RAN OVER MY FOOT

One thing's for certain: If you work at the mine, you'll eventually have an injury. My first injury happened while working in a unit with my guy friend and coworker, Sprinkles, whose father happened to be my chiropractor. On this day, we were standing beside the coal rib talking while I waited for my partner to bring the roof bolter over. I didn't notice that he was closing in on where I stood. Suddenly, I felt a force in my back and before I knew it, I was on the ground. My coworker had run into me from behind and knocked me down with the roof bolter! The tire ran over my foot, and I immediately felt a crushing pain shoot through my body as I tensed every fiber in my being to attempt to absorb the shock happening in my mind because of what was happening to my body. It was a never-ending moment. I didn't think he was ever going to stop. Sprinkles and I were screaming and yelling, and once he realized what was going on, he finally stopped. The pain pulsed through my body like a wave, and it was unbearable. I could feel it, I couldn't register the feeling but my whole body broke while holding together, it seemed. I could barely breathe, and I was in total shock as I pulled off my hard hat and scarf. I had never felt that kind of pain before in my life. I cried and screamed uncontrollably. As I clinched the air and spasmed, Sprinkles and my partner and the rest of the unit loaded me on the man trip and took me up top.

The mine manager was waiting for me when I got off the elevator. He heard me yelling and said, "Quit screaming, Tweety Bird! Your foot's not even broken." Oh Sure! I thought, Tell me anything! I stopped screaming and noticed that the ambulance was there waiting. Knowledge of help brings an odd comfort, but I was miserable. They transported me to Gibson General Hospital in Princeton, unloaded me from the ambulance into Emergency, where an E.R. Doctor saw me immediately. He looked at my x-rays and determined that my ankle was broken. I started crying all over again. I was then transported to Good Samaritan Hospital in Vincennes, which took another 30 minutes. I finally arrived and they gave me some pain meds. I went into surgery and had a screw placed in my ankle. I was later put into a full leg cast that started from the top of my thigh to the bottom of my ankle. I was in the hospital for over a week.

Since it was the summer, my doctor warned me that my leg would get hot, and that the cast would make me itch. I had to promise him that I would not stick a hanger or any objects in my cast to scratch my leg and I agreed. Two weeks later, my leg was dry, itchy, and driving me crazy. I found a metal hanger, bent it, and scratched away, not realizing the damage I was doing to the cast. A couple of weeks later, I got caught in the rain, which soaked my cast. I called the doctor to let him know what had happened and thankfully, he was able to get me in right away. He cut off the cast and when he noticed the damage from the hanger, he became immediately annoyed. He scolded and confronted me about sticking hangers inside. He was also annoyed that I was out in the rain. He replaced my cast and sent me on my way with a set of strict rules to follow. About three weeks later, I wanted to take a shower. I got the bright idea to wrap my leg with a trash bag. I taped the top, middle and the bottom. To me, it looked secure and waterproof, so I hobbled into the shower. I immediately began to slip and slide all over the place and before I knew it, my cast was drenched. I struggled to get up. Then I just laid there for a second, mad at myself. I was so disappointed and embarrassed to call the Doc again. When I finally got the courage to call, he barely said a word and the same thing happened when I went to his office for my appointment. He was cold, angry, and disgusted at my inability to follow simple instructions.

Three weeks had passed, and I was getting around well. At the time, I lived in an apartment and my place was on the third floor. I was getting used to hobbling up and down those long and narrow stairs with my crutches. One afternoon, I was leaving my apartment with my daughter, who was three at the time and still learning how to walk down the stairs, when she tumbled down the first step. I tried to break her fall with my crutch, but instead, I fell on top of her, and we tumbled down the steps together. I was in so much pain and I knew that I had broken my ankle again. I crawled up the steps with my daughter, went back inside, and called my doctor. When I finally got back to his office, he was livid. He told me he didn't ever want to see me again as he x-rayed my ankle. I was so relieved when the x-ray revealed that my ankle was not broken. He cut off my thigh cast and replaced it with a below-the-knee cast. Thankfully, I was able to move around more freely and keep my cast intact with no problems and no additional doctor's visits for 6 months, at which time the cast was removed, but unfortunately for him, due to the jarring pains in my ankle when the weather changed. I ended up needed to have surgery to get the screw removed.

WHICH SIDE ARE YOU ON?

M y ankle was finally healed and I was back to work and before I knew it, our contract was up it was time to go on strike again. The mine officials didn't agree to our demands for increased hourly pay, which we rightfully deserved. We risked our lives every day, which made our work specialized and worthy of the pay increase that we were demanding. We also wanted assurance that if something happened to us, our families would be taken care of. We waited for the company and the union to reach an agreement in vain. The mine owners and executives felt that we were paid too much as it was. It amazed me in fact, these mine administrators wanted to reduce our pay, without ever spending a day in our shoes. None of these men had ever stepped foot underground, so how could they begin to understand the dangers we faced daily. Thankfully, I was well prepared for this strike when it happened. Each month I paid into a strike fund, in addition to the union dues that we paid on a regular basis. This gave us some financial protection and the guarantee that we would still receive a paycheck while on strike.

We were sent to another mine on the first day of the strike, the signs had already been made for us. We picketed for hours, demanding equal pay and better amenities, and came up with a few catchy chants to get and keep morale high. It was a peaceful protest, which I was grateful for. I had heard that strikes in the past were quite different and even got hostile. The most extreme strike ended with the beatings and arrests of several mine employees. Fortunately, this did not happen to us. As the days and negotiations went on, the mine officials called in temp workers to keep the mine running. When the replacements, whom we referred to as "Scabs", came in, we would get in front of the gate as they entered and simply hold up our signs and yell at them. They were miners from other nearby mines after all and they were doing their job. Many of them were good people like us, but this didn't stop us from expressing our disdain and frustration. We knew business had to go on with or without us. Most of our anger wasn't even aimed at the replacements, it was at the ones who so easily showed us that we were replaceable.

The strike lasted two weeks, and once negotiations were reached, I happily returned to work. My bills had been piling up and the little "strike" check was not cutting it. The negotiations had been completed, and the union had accepted the company's offer, which included a pay raise and additional safety measures for miners' protection. The entire process was quite a learning experience. As union employees, we had to be willing to stand up for our rights and fight for the terms we wanted no matter how much our company wanted to take them away from us. In my opinion, the mine owners and leadership were just greedy, and we all worked too hard to allow them to get away with that. I believe in what the union does and have benefitted from its protections on more than one occasion. It saved my job more than once. I stand for what the union represents. It made a difference for me in my work life.

MOTORCYCLE MAMAS

There is something so freeing about riding motorcycles. This is especially liberating for women because stereotypically, riding bikes was a man's thing. Not so for my friend Sue and me. We met and worked at the same coal mine and even lived in the same little town. But our connection was sustained and nurtured through our love for riding motorcycles. Sue worked hard, she knew how to run the continuous mining machine and the roof bolter.

Sue had a Harley Davidson, and I had a Honda. Sue's bike was big. It was a 1974 Harley Davidson, 1200cc Shovelhead, fully dressed, and she could handle it. My bike, a Honda 750, was not as big or as nice as hers. I got into motorcycles while married to Mike and we had owned a bike together. My love for riding remained, even though our relationship fell apart. Riding bikes became me and Sue's thing and a way for us to blow all our cares and troubles to the wind. It felt good and gave me a sense of control and power, something I needed at that time in my life. It gave me the feeling of freedom.

Our bike rides also had other perks: It gained us admiration and respect from the guys at the job. They thought it was cool to see women riding motorcycles back and forth to work. They would stand there in amazement as Sue, and I rumbled into the parking lot with our bikes. We didn't ride for the attention or validation from anyone else. In a way, riding those bikes was like therapy and it gave us a break from life as single working mothers. Sue has three boys, who were young during this time. When we were on those bikes, nothing else mattered.

IT ALL FALLS DOWN

There's something that I learned early on at the mine that transferred over into my daily life: No matter what, you must do what must be done. You might not think you have the skills or knowledge to get it done, but strangely enough, when you commit to getting something done, it gets done. I knew nothing about masonry, yet this didn't stop my supervisor from requesting that I build a wall in one of the mine shafts. I had worked with some good masons over the years, who were responsible for building walls to direct the airflow within the mine. These walls were often made from bricks, and some were even constructed from tin. It seemed like an easy job if someone was there to help. I had a good friend, Irene, who was a mason and whom I had known for several years. One night I was assigned to work with her, and she worked circles around me. She would build two walls in one night while I struggled to complete one. Irene came from Kentucky, where she was a mine shooter. She worked with dynamite to blast open sections of coal, creating new places for miners to dig. She was a "bad mama jama". Irene had a reputation, all the miners from Kentucky talked about how good she was at what she did. She excelled at any job assigned to her. I enjoyed working and talking with her and I learned a lot from her vast skill set. But I did not like building walls.

When my supervisor asked me to build a wall, I had no idea that I'd be doing it by myself. We were short staffed that night which meant I'd have to figure it out alone. My boss could care less that I had never built a wall by myself. He just wanted it done. He simply told me to take my time and get it done before my shift was over. Talk about pressure. I grabbed a piece of material and got to work. I did my best to mimic what I had seen Irene do as I worked through the shift, putting pieces of the wall together. About six hours later, I was done. I took a step back and marveled at my work. I was proud and it felt good to take on this task by myself. I went to go get my boss so he could see my work. You should've seen the look of pride I had in my eyes, until I found out that the wall had collapsed while I was gone. Every piece was on the ground, laying haphazardly as if I never worked on it in the first place. I was embarrassed and my boss was annoyed. I didn't realize that I had to "cat board" it by placing a piece of wood at the top, cata-cornered to the wall, which would have prevented the wall from falling. My boss jumped in and helped me rebuild the wall and left once I had a pretty good hang of it. Even with the mishap, I managed to finish the wall before my shift was over and I could officially say that I knew how to build a wall on my own.

On another occasion, I was assigned to work a unit with a girlfriend and our task was to build a wall from tin. Since we were good friends, I just knew the night would be fun and easy. We spotted the tin and slowly dragged the pieces to the area where we were to build the wall. I leaned the tin against my chest and positioned it against an opposite wall. I looked down and something was smeared all over the front of my shirt and at first glance, it looked like chocolate. Unfortunately, it was not. It was not chocolate. Unbeknownst to me, someone had pooped on the tin, and it was all over my shirt. It was not a good look for me. I had desperately hoped it was candy until I caught a whiff of the smell, and it made me sick. My friend didn't even realize that I had gotten into some poop. When she finally looked up at me, the only thing I could say was, "I thought it was chocolate!" We both fell out into thunderous laughter.

After that, I was extra vigilant of where I sat and was careful when touching anything. It was crazy because seeing poop was such a common thing in the mine. Although there were portable buckets for us to use as bathrooms, no one wanted to go through the hassle of locating the buckets, using them, then cleaning them out. It was just too much. Although I understood why some people thought it best to just "pop a squat" where they were at; it was still gross and highly unsanitary. I called our mine manager so that he could take me up top to take a shower and change my clothes. After I cleaned up, I returned to my unit, and we continued to work on the wall. Thankfully we finished the night without any other hiccups and the "chocolate" remained our little secret.

DEALING WITH DEATH

L osing someone you love is never easy. That pain is compounded when two people you love, grew up with, who played a major part in your upbringing transition around the same time. For nearly a week, I had been going back and forth to the hospital to visit my aunt Annie, my grandmother's sister, who was very ill. My grandmother had passed earlier in the year, and I was still healing from and coming to grips with her passing when my aunt Annie became ill. My aunt Annie and grandmother were so close, and my aunt often mentioned how much she missed her sister. She missed talking to her, which they did every day. I looked up to my aunt because she was my spiritual role model. She loved God and it showed through her actions and her generous heart. Aunt Annie could also make a mean dandelion wine, something that I would help her with when I was younger by picking the dandelions from her backyard. Aunt Annie worked hard and appreciated the beauty all around her. Her garden was filled with flowers of every variety, the perfect oasis to escape to after a long day of work or to get lost in while playing hide and seek with cousins.

I was at work when one of the girls told me that I was wanted in the front office. I was told it was an emergency. I was already underground and knew it was serious because they never brought us to the top. It was around 8 a.m. and the shift admin was in the office. Once I reached the office, I was handed the phone. It was a nurse from the hospital. My aunt had passed away. The office walls felt like they were caving in on me, and I immediately felt a deep, familiar pain resurface from my heart. The tears flowed profusely from my eyes. There was no way I was going back underground after that news, so I stayed in the office for my last hour and cried. I couldn't stop feeling or thinking that my aunt Annie had died of a broken heart.

When my grandmother passed away, I did not go to work for almost a whole month. I stayed in bed and cried. I didn't eat and I barely moved. The human resources representative told me that I had to see a psychiatrist. When I went, he asked me if I had something to talk about. I could not say anything. I did not know him, and I knew that he did not know me or my grandmother. The visit with him did not make me feel any better. My best friend Ardella would come over and visit and get me to do things, like clean my house. I had let everything go. I would hate to see her coming. She would say, "Come on B, get out of this bed. We are going to clean this house." I wanted to tell her to go home, but I knew I could not. My Grandmother would have been very unhappy with me. We had talked about her dying before her death. She would say to me, "Janice, what are you going to do when I die?' I told her I hoped to go before her. She said, "You damn fool, I have lived my life. You have yours to live for." She said, "but I am going to die, and you will make it."

There had been one death after another in our family, but none took me down like my grandmother's. She was my heart, my lifeline, my reason. I mourned her passing and with time, I slowly came back around. I would hear my father's wisdom replaying in my mind that the Davison's were tough people. I also knew I had to pull it together for my children; they were depending on me, and I couldn't let them or my grandmother down. My aunt Annie's death reopened the wound of my grandmother's death for me, and I felt that same familiar pain. It was hard, yet what gave me a glimmer of hope was knowing that both my grandmother and aunt were reunited and would get to talk every day again.

After losing the two most important women in my life, I decided to settle down with John, the man I was dating after my divorce. I didn't want to be alone, so I spent a lot of time with him in Princeton, and later became pregnant.

EVERY 15 MINUTES

When I was eight months pregnant with my third child, I was extremely tired. I had previously suffered two miscarriages while working underground and did not want to lose this baby. My doctor was from India, and I was not sure if she knew what my job was. I tried to tell her, but she did not speak English too well. At this time, I was roof bolting full time and worked a nine-hour shift. I would leave my house at 10:30 p.m., get to the mine around 11 p.m., and mentally prepare to go underground, starting my shift at midnight. I stayed underground until 9:00 a.m., would go home and rest, then do it all over again the next night.

My doctor had me come into her office every week to get iron shots. I did not care for that at all. My feet would swell up and I always had to pee but there wasn't a bathroom close by. I would need to go to the next crosscut, which meant I was squatting down and peeing on the coal. Imagine my pregnant self, trying to get down low and find a place to pee quietly. I hoped no one would walk by and see me. This happened every 15 minutes, all night long. Running the roof bolter was hard on me. My roof bolter partner had asked me when I was going to stop working. I said that my doctor would not let me off. I was so embarrassed about the whole thing. My girlfriend, Sue, was worried about me. She feared that I was going to miscarry underground. Sue asked me if she could call my doctor. I don't know what she said but a couple of days later my doctor called and asked me to come into her office. When I arrived, she apologized and handed me the paperwork for me to start my maternity leave. If it wasn't for my girlfriend, I probably would have lost my baby. I am beyond grateful that Jesus sent me an angel known as Sue. I know my partner was finally glad that I would be off. He probably hated my doctor and me, too. My feet hurt and I always had to go to the bathroom, which slowed our progress. Thankfully, he never complained and remained kind to me. My bosses were patient as well.

RUNAWAY BOLTER

I had just gotten back from maternity leave and I was assigned to replace bolts on the track bolter. My partner noticed we were out of supplies and that we needed bolts, roof plates, and glue. He left to get the supplies, so I stayed behind to start the setup, which included moving the roof bolter to the work area. Roof bolters are machines that are used to drive steel rods into the mine roof, anchoring into outlying rock, to help keep the material in place. I hopped off the roof bolter but failed to put the brakes all the way down. The bolter started to move down the hill fast. Once I realized what was happening, I started running after it and eventually caught up with it after running for about 10 feet. I immediately shut it off. I was panting and sweating profusely. When I looked up, I noticed that my manager was looking straight at me. He was laughing hysterically. "You know that you must put the brakes on the machine," he said before scolding me about safety. I was embarrassed and scared. It was one of those moments that everyone who operates equipment or machinery must experience at least one time in some minor or major way. Thankfully this was not major, but it could have been, and no one got hurt but Lord knows what could have been.

My heart was racing. I often did silly things that would get me in trouble, mainly because I didn't know what I was doing and was learning along the way. If I did the job more than once, I was able to catch on, but I didn't work the roof bolter often, so it was easy to forget how to use it. It slipped my mind that once I parked the bolter; I needed to ensure that the emergency brakes were on. Believe me, I never forgot that again. I would check the brakes, recheck the brakes. Then I'd check again.

Our mine used a fleet of 22 continuous mining machines to remove the coal. The machines load the coal into shuttle cars. The shuttle cars move to haul trucks used in surface mines but also used underground to transport coal from the continuous mining machines to conveyor belts that carry the coal to the surface. It's quite the process of human and machine dominos falling and resetting. A dusty clockwork.

I enjoyed running the roof bolter after working with it for several days. It was a lot different than being in a unit and trying to keep up with the continuous mining.

It was a less stressful job even though it had its stressful moments. I considered myself a good roof bolter and wanted to be as good as the men. I wanted them to trust me and have confidence that I could do the job. I know a lot of guys did not like me in the beginning, but I quickly earned their respect. Just like that grumpy old man in the nursing home. It made me feel good about myself when the bosses started telling me how good I was. I began to feel like I could really do this job. There were only a handful of women roof bolters, which made me feel like I had to prove myself as a woman roof bolter. I'm sure I was not the only woman who felt that way.

ROCK DUSTER MOTOR-MAMA

When women slack on the job, it's never a good look. This meant that as a female miner, I always had to work 10 times harder. This was true for all the women miners and we each did our best to do our best. We didn't want to give anyone a reason to say, "See, this is why mining isn't for women." I had a co-worker named Moochie who I'd often worked the third shift with. I did not like working with Moochie. It was always laziness with her, and she did not understand what it meant to work as a team. My partner and I were assigned to work with her.

On the weekends the mine did not produce coal so we dedicated the entire shift to cleaning out "glob and rock", so production can continue freely without any backups.

 Moochie worked as a rock duster motor-man, or in this case, motor-woman. She would run the machine and tend to the motor, hence the job title, and I was a rock duster, responsible for dusting the coal mine. We dusted the mines for basic fire prevention. Coal is highly flammable, and the white powder that we dusted in the mine helped keep the coal from igniting. We covered everything: the rocks, walls, the roof, the floor, and anything in between. Moochie's job was to stay at the machine so she could control the gauges and keep the pressure steady for the entire shift.

Rock dusters were not only responsible for dusting but cleaning up the rocks and debris from the previous week, then preparing the area for the coming week. The rock duster machine ran along an underground track and Moochie was responsible for running it. The dust traveled down a large pipe that extended above ground, into the machine, which was then carried through the attached hose to the nearest area that needed rock dusting. Moochie would stop the machine on the tracks as close as possible to the area needing the dust, then I would turn the machine on to blow the dust out through long tubes that extend out about 1,000 feet. She could adjust the pressure to low, medium, or high and she was responsible for watching the gauge. Her job was to ensure the pressure was not blowing too hard through the long hose.

When the mine manager informed Dandy and I that we would be working with the rock duster motorman, we started preparing early so that when Moochie arrived, we would be ready. We took out the rock dusting hoses and started to lock everything into place. The mine manager also wanted to ensure the area was pretty and white. We were ready with our hoses, so by the time Moochie arrived, all that was left to do was connect the hoses to the machine. We used old rock dust hoses and when the hoses got to her, they were packed with dust from the previous shift. We shook the hoses out as much as we could then dragged them to put them in place.

Once we were ready, we told Moochie to give us about 15 minutes to make it back to the dusting spot before she turned the machine on. I was in the front, holding the hose near the spray, and my partner was behind me. He supported the hose by holding it and pulling the hose back. I held the end of the hose to direct the dust spray around the beltline to make sure it was pretty and white. We would start from the farthest point and slowly walk backwards as I covered everything in our path with dust. As I backed up, Dandy pulled the hose back to help me control it. Suddenly, the hose began to wildly spray with such force that it flipped me back and forth, like a rag doll, then knocked me down under the belt. I started coughing uncontrollably. I am sure I looked like an angry anaconda blowing dust in every direction. I had rock dust in my eyes, ears, and nose. I could not see anything. My partner had to take my hand and lead me to a safe place. I retrieved my eye cleanser so I could see where I was going, then we made our way over to Moochie to see what was going on. When we finally got to her, she was asleep at the wheel! Apparently, while she was sleeping, she accidentally turned the pressure to 'high.' I wanted to knock her out. I was blessed that I did not get hurt. As a consolation, I was the motor-woman for the rest of the shift, and my partner and sleeping beauty went back to the undusted area to finish the job. When our manager came back to check on us, he saw that we got the job done and that was the only thing that mattered to him. He never knew what happened that night.

PRANKS IN THE MINES

W e found a way to keep things light and fun although we were doing serious work underground. However, there were times when those pranks and jokes took a left turn. On one occasion, we were getting on the elevator to go home when one of the guys decided to play a joke on one of my close girlfriends, Viola. We called her Vi for short. She was from Kentucky and a joy to be around. I loved to hear her talk just to hear her accent. The guys knew that she did not like mice and the mine was full of them.

A few of the guys knew what the one guy was up to. The cage held about 50 people at a time and even with the maximum number of people it was still tight. The guy told Vi to look at his hands. He showed her the baby mice. She grabbed him, knocked them down, and the baby mice went everywhere. The cage was already crowded and somehow, Vi pushed her way through to the back of the cage, screaming the whole time. She grabbed people and pulled them in front of her. She was screaming so loud that I thought she was going to hurt herself before the doors opened. Of course, the little mice did not make it. They got stepped on. Vi was terrified and she was a mess. The guy who brought the mice was bleeding from her scratching and beating him. I felt a little sorry for the guy. He was black and blue for a good week.

A bunch of people got hurt that day. I was just trying to stay standing up. The cage door couldn't open soon enough. The guy who brought in the mice never tried it again. Vi was not faking; she did not like mice. If I had known what was going to happen that day, I would have waited for the next cage. I would have reacted in a similar way if that had been a spider. But I sure did not let the guys know about that or any of my fears. I don't know how they found out about her fear. They may have seen her running from them, or she may have told them herself, never thinking anyone would do something that sinister.

Shortly after the mice situation, we had another prank. This time, a smelly one. I didn't have a clue as to why the cage smelled so horrible sometimes. It was so bad that you would not want to breathe until you got off. The cage lacked circulation which meant there wasn't any fresh air. It was hard to hold your breath to keep the bad smell out; you were going to get a whiff of it sooner or later, somehow someway anyway. Sometimes the smell seemed to get stronger and stronger. Everyone would try to rush out of the cage once above ground just to inhale fresh air. After some investigating, we finally found out what the smell was. A guy would bring a pill or capsule on the cage then step on it, releasing that horrid smell. Racid, really. He wasn't the only person who did this, and they did this quite often. I smelled more of it than I care to say, and it was just plum nasty. It made me feel sick knowing that I could not go anywhere without smelling it. I wanted them to keep the doors open so badly. I never knew that you could buy stuff like that, but someone in the mine sure did. I guess that they thought it would spice it up. Correction, they wanted to stink it up. I could have done without it. I am sure a lot of us felt that way. Sometimes you just wanted to get back to the top, take your shower, and just go home. I had been involved in some of the horseplay before, but I could've gone without the stinky bombs. It didn't make any sense to me. The same people who brought the stinky bombs also had to smell it, but it didn't seem to bother them.

Our underground dining hole was one of the nicer ones; it was surrounded by coal. We put thick plastic around the area to keep the dust out and keep it clean. When we ordered supplies, the men would purchase lumber and make picnic tables and chairs to sit on. Every unit was different, depending upon the people and the boss. You could tell a lot about each unit based on their dinner hole. It was like a red flag about the boss and the people who worked in that unit.

One day I went to the hole for my 30-minute break. As I walked through the plastic, I almost stepped on a mouse as it ran in front of me. When I noticed the mouse, he was running in circles with his tail cut off. I looked up and there were mice hanging upside down from the plastic. Each mouse had been skinned. I was terrified. When the men saw my reaction, they cracked up laughing. They apparently got a kick out of it all. Although I did not particularly like mice, I felt this was a bit much. We ate and rested in that dinner hole area, after all, so I didn't understand how they could be so disgusting. I was glad I did not step on any mice. The whole thing was just sad and foul. To this day, I still cannot fathom the cruelty some of the men were capable of, all for the sake of a joke. Sadistic by any means. I think the men just wanted to see my reaction, but I did not give them any satisfaction. I acted as though the mice did not bother me and I continued as if nothing happened.

There was never a dull moment. The guys always came up with weird pranks to keep us all on our toes at the mine. They once decided to put grease in the earpiece of the dining hole phone. The old coal miners knew not to use the phone without checking it first, but the newbies had no idea. Grease is sticky and slippery and makes dust stick to you like glue. It is annoying and it makes your ear feel filthy. We were always covered in coal dust and when you tried to wipe the grease off with your hand, you just smeared coal across your ears. If you tried to use your shirt, then you were wiping more dirt and dust into your ear. So, by the time you were done, there was grease on your ear, the side of your face, your hand, and your clothes. It was irritating to get all that grease all over you with no paper towels, restrooms, or towelettes to clean up with. You would have to go around with grease on you through your entire shift.

I was in one unit and the boss got his ear greased. As you would guess, he was really upset about it. No one said a word. Even when our jobs were threatened, we would not say a word. We called ourselves family, which meant we did not snitch on each other. We were a union and that is the way we operated. Together we stood and together we fell. Whether the joke involved a boss or a coworker, you had to be a part of it. That was one of the unwritten rules of union relationships. I do not remember too much going on that would have caused the mine any real liability. It was just good ole, mean spirited fun. I am sure a few people did not enjoy it at all. Some of it was a little too much, even for me, but believe me, I could laugh with the rest of them if I had to. I did not laugh so much when it was on me. I remember wanting to get them back, but I just could not think of anything. That was not my normal way of operating. I was just so busy with work and home, so plotting jokes and pranks wasn't my top priority. I had other more important things that occupied my thoughts and time. I saw so much in the coal mine. It was not just the coal miners doing pranks, we also had some sneaky bosses who'd get in on the fun. They liked a good laugh, too.

BIG PANTIES

There was a small room to the right of the mine, right before the top ramp. The company that ran the coal mine had different things in it over the years. I remember it being a room for medical supplies. If you needed a Band-Aid or got something in your eyes, you would go into that room to get it. I heard that some mines had on-call nurses, but ours did not. We just had the medical room. The company gave us a medical supply box to keep with us. They would make sure it was full. On the wall, they had a board. Some of the guys who liked a good joke, had a sign up that read: Are these yours? They were referring to a big pair of panties. They had put them on the board with the sign underneath them. It was the biggest pair of women's panties I had ever seen. They had pinned them high so that everyone could see them.

I did not know one woman at the mine that had a butt that big. They stayed up for about a day. The company finally took them down. But they laughed about it, too. That was one of the few harmless jokes at the mine. I suppose I could have been offended that it was women's panties and not some trousers, but I was more relieved that they were not mine. I would have been embarrassed if they were. I would have never told a soul. I would have just kept on going like I had no idea. You always knew that any joke in the mine could turn on you. It amazed me the steps that the guys and girls would take for a good joke underground. It made the shift go a lot faster and sometimes got our minds off some of the dangerous and stressful situations around us.

I was in the bath house, coming out of the shower butt naked and minding my own business, when one of the women goosed, me by pinching me on my butt. I felt violated. I was so caught off guard that I jumped. I tried to run away but instead I ran smack into the wall. If I could have, I would have turned red. I did not like being naked in front of everyone. We had some women who enjoyed watching other women shower. I was told that the woman who goosed me, liked women, but I did not care about that. I figured that was her business. As long as she left me alone, I didn't care who she liked. But when she decided to touch me, she crossed the line. As I stood there in pain, she was laughing her head off.

"What the heck do you think you're doing?!" I asked her sharply. She kept laughing.

"If you just coulda' seen your face going into the wall!" she said carelessly.

"It's not funny, you coulda' caused me a heart attack," I snapped back. I knew that I did not have anything to worry about. She just thought she was being cute. She even asked me the next day if I was trying to kiss the wall. There was never a dull moment with her around. I was not going to lie, it scared me a little and I was angry. My whole body was shaking, but all in all, she was a good person who just needed to get her laugh on. It took me until the next day to be able to laugh about it though. Afterward as I took a Woosah in the shower, I thought "silly girl" and chuckled while also angry. The juxtaposition of life will make you laugh and cry at the same thing sometimes.

The jokes and pranks didn't end with those panties or being goosed. I had a coworker who made it his business to target people. Bobby always played jokes on people just to get a laugh. Not a laugh for us but for himself. He played a joke on everyone, on this occasion, he set his sights on an older woman named Fertie. Fertie was in her early 60s and she worked on the belt head. I never understood why she never got on a unit. At times, she seemed a bit bitter about her position. There were other times she seemed paranoid about her equipment. Some people thought she was off, but I believe she had better sense than she let on. Some days, she was hot and some days she was cold. We never knew if she was going to be nice, or just plain ole mad. I still liked her though.

One night, the mine manager had Fertie on one of the belt heads, cleaning the area. Bobby knew that she was down there alone in the dark working. Bobby was also working on the belt head in a different section. I believe this was a Saturday and usually there were not as many bosses watching on that day, so he probably figured it was the best opportunity to get his joke on. He was young and was always doing something crazy and this time he had this ghostly-looking Halloween mask. From what I was told, he put that silly mask on, quietly snuck up behind Fertie, and started running as fast as he could, like a ghost coal miner seeking bloody revenge. I could only imagine what that poor old lady must have thought when she heard fast footsteps approaching her. Bobby was well-built and probably appeared to be a dark and swift demon. Once she turned around to look back over her shoulder, there is no telling what she could have thought seeing a ghost face of death. As the story was told, she took off running so fast that her hard hat flew off her head, hit the ground, and bounced behind her off the rocks, dragging behind her by the battery cord.

"Oh Jesus, help me! Oh Lord!" He heard her yelling, as she ran. I would not wish that type of fear on anybody and I am sure that her little heart was filled with terror.

"Fertie, it's me!" Bobby said as he realized that his stupid joke had turned deadly. Fertie was running in the dark, very close to the belt without her light.

"Fertie!!" He continued to yell to her as he kept running to try to catch her.

She was so fast that he could barely keep up. I heard that at this point Bobby got scared because he realized she could really get hurt if he was not able to stop her.

"It's me, Bobby!" he said when he finally caught up to her and grabbed her arm.

Who knows why she did not slap him after being grabbed by that silly boy, but she finally stopped! I would have hurt him, but she did not. Strangely enough, she liked that kid and was willing to forgive him instead of reporting him. In addition, she had no animosity towards him. I would have reported him and tried to think of a way to get back at him. The most unbelievable part of the entire prank was how fast she ran. Bobby was shocked about that, too. He had played a joke on me once and I was thinking that if she was as scared as I was angry, Bobby could have made Fertie have a heart attack. I understood the humor and laughed when I first heard about it, mainly because we knew how certifiably crazy Bobby was. After that prank though, Bobby stopped doing crazy things to people.

SCREAMING "BENNY" IN MY BED

I was once assigned to an all-male unit with a good group of people on third shift. Benny was the boss in charge. He was a family man with a wife and two kids. Our crew liked having him for a boss. I enjoyed being around all of them because they believed in God and all of us got along well and respected one another. Benny taught Sunday School. Another guy said he was a preacher and all of us belonged to a church and, at that time I served as a children's choir director at my church. We were all on the same page. Benny loved a good joke and sometimes, it was my turn to be on the receiving end. It was lunchtime and I was ready for my 30 minutes to sit down and rest. I was so tired that when I got to the dinner hole, I fell asleep shortly after sitting. When I sat down, I had the nerve to sit right across from Benny. Unfortunately for me, he had a huge wad of tobacco in his mouth and at that moment, he decided to spit a mouthful of stinky tobacco right on my bottom lip. I woke up so fast, spitting and coughing at the same time. "I bet you will stay awake from now on," he said, pleased with himself. Everyone laughed. I was so mad when I found out what was in my mouth. I wanted to choke him. I was grossed out by the fact that something on my lip had come from his mouth. I got so sick knowing that his saliva had been on my lip that I felt nauseous. I never did anything to get back at him. I remember thinking of many things but none of them were worth losing my job for. He was still the boss, after all. To him and the guys, it was a good joke.

It was a Friday night and I fell into a deep sleep. John said I woke up screaming, "Stop Benny, stop!" He wanted to know who the hell Benny was, so I had to tell him the story. When I got back to work, I told my boss that he was going to get me killed. He started laughing again.

MY HAIR IS MY CROWN AND COVERING

There were two things I didn't play about: My daily shower and my hair. The only time we skipped showers was when the hot water went out in the cold of winter. When I worked a long shift, I would be sweaty and full of dust and dirt. My face would be black covered with soot. I never wanted to get that mess in my car. Even after a good cleaning you could still see the speckle of coal dust and that smell would linger in the air. The few times I had to skip my shower I would pray that I didn't have to stop for any reason. I was certain that if anyone saw me, they wouldn't recognize me. The soot would even get into my nose making my mucus black. The "coal shower" ensured that I really felt clean and refreshed after a hard day's work underground.

The women's shower room could sometimes be a little weird. It was like a high school P.E. Class and there was that initial awkwardness of showering in front of other girls. When I was in high school, I didn't want anyone to look at my body. I am sure the other girls felt the same way. It was called growing up. I initially felt a little funny about it, but I knew it had to be done, so I just accepted it.

It still feels awkward when I go to the gym and women look my way when I am either putting on or taking off my clothes. Yes, I know no one is paying attention to me. When I was in high school my body looked good, but I still didn't want anyone to see me naked. A lot has changed with my body since then. You can also say I'm mainly concerned about violation of privacy, especially with the current trend of cell phones and the internet. I don't want to see my naked body on the internet or a picture of me being passed around the gym. This might sound extreme, but this very thing happened at the mine once.

It was during one of the shifts when I worked at portal one, and had to use their showers, which weren't as nice as the ones at portal two. Portal, one had less shower stalls, which meant that we all had to take turns to use the shower. I never liked to work on that side of the mine for this reason. On this one occasion, we were standing around waiting for our turn to take a shower. Some of the women had towels on while others were completely naked. The next thing I knew, one of my silly co-workers decided that she was going to take some pictures. I don't know why she thought that was okay and that she would get away with it, but she got her feelings hurt fast, because one of my friends grabbed the camera out of her hands and broke it in front of her. She was so surprised and didn't seem to understand why her camera had been broken. She was very lucky that the other women were so tired and did not do something worse, because she could have quite easily got more than her camera broken. I couldn't believe she thought we would be alright with her taking photos of us naked, but obviously she thought wrong. We were angry and even though she was also a woman, we all felt violated. I never asked her why she did what she did, but I learned later that one of the other miners had put her up to it, which I really didn't believe at the time. I'm glad my girlfriend snatched the camera from her. That was the last time she brought a camera into the mine again. Knowing the full Monty, I felt vindicated.

The Bible says in I Corinthians 11:15 that "if a woman has long hair, it is a glory to her; for her hair is given to her for a covering." I like my covering. My co-workers probably thought that I didn't have any hair. I always wore a scarf on my head. The scarf was a big handkerchief, and I wore a stocking cap underneath it. The cap went on first to keep my hair in place, then I would tie the scarf tight so that my hair would stay in place all night and day.

Black hair is all about maintenance. Back then, I had a hairdresser who lived an hour away and I could only see him once a month. He charged a lot for a relaxer. The whole process took a full day from planning my babysitter, to driving and finally, the long wait in a busy salon. One time I fell asleep for 20 minutes while under the hair dryer. I was completely "out of the hood". All the girls in the salon were cracking up and when I woke up, I was so embarrassed. I was exhausted by the time I made it home, but my hair looked good. Black hair is an investment and a societal sacrifice. I started to learn how to braid my own hair by doing my daughter's hair. I would add synthetic hair to mine so the braids would be thicker and last longer. My braids would last me a couple of months. I was once coming out of the shower when one of my synthetic hair braids fell out. One of the girls had picked it up off the floor and folded it over my basket. Once I noticed, I laughed quietly to myself as I had not even noticed that a braid had fallen out.

DON'T LET THEM KNOW

The manager of the coal mine was a man's man by every definition of the word. He was a great person and there weren't very many people who did not like him. If you did your job, you were good on his list. There was one thing about him, however: He had a weak stomach. He did not want to hear any talk of blood or things of that nature. I figured this out during the time I had a miscarriage underground. "Don't say anything, Tweety bird" he said firmly when he came to get me. He did not want a description of what happened or a visual picture of what my body went through. He just simply stated, "Tweety bird, do what you have to do," and that was it. The men would talk bad about him. Everyone knew about it unless you were new at the mine. The word was out, and the men got together and decided that they would play a joke on him. Somehow, they got a sanitary napkin, poured ketchup on it, and hung it from his car. When he got off work, he went to his car, saw the napkin hanging from the antenna and immediately vomited. In the mines, you just could not let people know your weakness. If the wrong person found out, it could be bad for you. In this case, it was our boss and his weak stomach fell victim.

The boss had a brother who worked with us. I suspect that he may have told the wrong person inadvertently or on purpose you never know. He probably thought that they would get a good laugh out of it, but I am sure that the boss did not think it was funny. Our mine manager was big, he was about 6'2", rough, with a scratchy looking beard and probably weighed around 250 pounds, you would never think that he would be afraid of blood, bugs, or gooey things. We all had respect for him regardless. He kept the third shift running and that is saying a lot. You sure had to know what you were doing to run a shift smoothly. He was one of the good ones.

TWO BULLIES

One time a group of men were all talking in the dinner hole, waiting around for everyone to get to the mantrap shuttle and go home. A couple of them hassled me about bringing in food. There was an unspoken requirement for any new person to bring food. I brought pigs in a blanket before. "Tweety Bird", you know you are supposed to bring something in, right?" one of the guys said.

"Yeah, we would like to put in an order," the other one chimed in.

"I already bought something once before," I said dismissively. "...and I am not going to bring anything else." I remembered wondering who they thought they were.

"You know, we could get some paint and paint you..." one guy started in.

"Yeah, or we could tie you up..." the other said.

"If you do, all of you will be in so much trouble," I retorted. A few of them laughed.

It was little ole me against a unit of Goliaths. I started talking so much stuff at that point. I am not sure what I was thinking. I did understand that in a world of men that if you did not learn to stick up for yourself or hang with the worst of them, you would get run over all the time. The next thing I knew, a bunch of them grabbed me and tied me up around the rib board with black mechanic tape. I guess they figured they would teach me a lesson. I screamed and fought but they were a lot stronger than me. They laughed and asked, "What was that you were gonna do? You ain't so tough now." I was upset. I couldn't believe they tied me up. They turned my light off. I could not move, and I could not say a word. Our boss walked right by me and did not see me. I could hear him ask, "Where's Tweety bird?" once they all got to the mantrap shuttle. No one said a word. He did come back to find me tied up and taped up. He untied me and laughed about it. The pranks happened so often that no one thought they were unusual; it was part of that underground life. I learned not to say a word after that. They made me believe that they were capable of doing more harm than I could ever imagine. It was only funny because they did not hurt me.

ADRIAN, MY HELP

My eldest son Adrian affectionately refers to me as his sister-mom. I was just a baby when I had him, which meant that we grew up together, learned together, and struggled together. If I were to label my oldest, I would call him my help. John and I depended on him a lot. He was the best helper, and he did a good job. While I was working third shift, he was the one to keep everything running smoothly at home. Adrian never complained. He knew what needed to be done and he seemed content to do it and he did it well. He was just as good with his baby sister and baby brother. He always seemed happy to please me. He would say, "I help my mother out," or "I did what she wanted me to do." In retrospect, I do not feel it was right for me to put so much responsibility on him. I knew my oldest would not let me down and I am forever grateful for him. I'm not sure how our family would have managed without him. I love all my children and I see a little of me in them. My youngest two were just too young at the time to really help much while me and John were working. They were busy being kids. I know working full time on the third shift was hard on all of them, but we got through it. As a family, we pulled it together. We loved each other hard, and I needed all the help that I could get.

I PROMISE

A s a child, my youngest son, Little John, never wanted to leave my side. I would get him ready for daycare and he would plead with me every morning to stay home. The daycare was at a well-known local church. I knew it was a great daycare because my daughter went there, and many coworkers had children there. Little John did not want any part of it. He just wanted to be with me. During this time, I was still on third shift and all I wanted to do was go to sleep during the day. I was getting home from work around 9 a.m. and I was beat. I would get Little John to school and as soon as he saw the parking lot, he would start crying, "Mama please... I will be a good boy. I just want to stay with you."

Sometimes I gave in, and I would bring him home and put on a movie. He would lay in the bed with me and watch his movie or play Pac-Man. He really was a good boy. On the days I made him stay at the daycare, it must have been hilarious to see; that boy had me jumping from one side to the other trying to open the car door and drag him out. I would be on one side and his teacher on the other. I can laugh about it now, but back then I was so tired that it took every ounce of patience for me to remain calm. Then there were the days where he would grab on to my leg and hold on for life. He would squeeze my leg so tightly that I had to pry him off as I walked. I started asking him questions. I wondered if they were mistreating my baby or hurting him at the daycare. He always said no, and I even met with the teachers to make sure they were supportive of my son and helping him learn. I did not realize at that time how much I was gone from our home, and how my work schedule affected him and all my kids. It was a lot for any child.

OPEN TO THE PUBLIC

The coal mine's anniversary was the first opportunity I had to bring my family in to see where I worked. I was excited, and since it was the anniversary, the mine leadership told us they were going to go all out. They did just that! They catered our lunch and fed us hotdogs, hamburgers, chips, soda, and a cookie. They gave each of the kids a bag so they could collect coal at the end of the tour. My family was so thrilled. They were finally going to see where I worked. John and my two youngest children, Myca, and Little John were there. The coal mine looked like a completely different place. It was so clean and pretty as a picture.

Everything was covered in rock dust, which made it look off white. I did not recognize this place at all, which was a good thing. I did not want my family to see what the coal mine looked like on a regular day. My family got to see the machines and the roof bolter I worked on. They had us in small groups with a guide to tell us about the coal mine history, the equipment and how it was used, the daily operations of the mine, and what the coal was for. At one point when our guide stopped talking, Little John, who was learning how to pee on his own, started peeing on the rocks. The look on some of the other people's faces was priceless. I thought they were going to take off running. Thank God he was standing behind me at that time. Our guide said, "Yes, that is how we do it. Just find a good place and relieve yourself".

DIET PILLS FOR WORK

It was a good thing that the mine did not conduct regular drug tests as many of us would have been out of work. I took all kinds of prescribed drugs over the years and so did some of the other miners. I needed most of those prescriptions to help relieve the pain and issues in my back, which had only gotten worse the longer I stayed at the mine. When working in the mines, you learn all kinds of tricks to help you stay alert and do well on the job. One of those tips was diet pills. I, along with three other girlfriends, would take diet pills to help with drowsiness. We all shared a doctor who was located close to the mine. We nicknamed him "Dr. Feelgood." The doctor was an older gentleman who was friendly; he never said no to our requests for more diet pills. I'm not sure if he was close to retiring or just didn't care.

I was very small at the time and only weighed about 118 pounds. I would take one pill right before we went underground. One night I had taken my pill before I went down and after getting dressed, I was told we were "striking" and that I had to go home. Once I got home, I attempted to go to sleep. My heart started to race; it seemed like my heart was beating out of my chest. I was so scared I could not sleep. I began to pray and asked God for his help. I know we're not supposed to bargain with God but in that moment, I felt I had no other option. "Lord, if you get me out of this, I will never do it again!" I said attempting to speak with God earnestly. I laid there for hours with my eyes wide open.

I thought I was going to have a heart attack. I never took diet pills again. I was so thankful that God had heard my prayer. I never wanted to go through that; that feeling kept me from doing any kind of hard drugs. From that point forward, I made sure that I got more rest so that I would not fall asleep at work. Everybody at home really tried to help me stay on my strict schedule. I had never been on a schedule before. I tried to make dinner or have something to eat for the kids when they came home from school. My daughter was old enough to feed herself and her baby brother. Then they would do homework, watch television, and play quietly. Most of the time that worked. Then there were the days I was awakened up by the sound of two kids yelling and fighting. John worked the second shift, and when he was away, those days were rough. The phone was constantly ringing from salespeople, friends, and family. The Jehovah Witness would stop by and ring the doorbell. And then there were my neighbors cutting their grass and my dogs barking. So much for sleep and my schedule. One thing is for certain: I stayed away from those diet pills. Once you intend a thing, the world comes to test that resolve.

THE KENTUCKY MEN

There were about four men who had been laid off from their mine in Kentucky and our company was accepting applications. They were all industrious workers and nice guys. The commute for them was about three hours when we had pleasant weather. My girlfriend who came from that same mine knew all of them. She said they all had big, beautiful homes. These guys were smart; they pooled their money together and bought a vehicle, so they could carpool together and took turns driving. It seemed to work out well for them. They never missed a day of work. They got along with everybody.

One night as they were on their way to work, one of the guys who liked to smoke cigars was driving. He threw his cigar out the window, but unfortunately, it did not go out of the window. Instead, it flew into the back seat of the car. No one was paying attention. They all walked away and worked a full shift. Nine hours later, we all discovered together that the car had burned up. There was no car for them to get back home with. The only thing that remained was a black frame and smoke; it smelled terrible. I heard the union helped them get home that day. These guys were determined, and they all showed up on time the next day for work. I was impressed. They had pooled their money together again and this time they bought a station wagon. When work is worth working past the costly mistake, you get back to work as soon as possible. When it means bread on the family's table, you do what it takes.

CARPOOL HELL

I have had my share of carpooling. In my day, carpooling was called catching a ride or just riding. Some rides were good, and some were not. It was common courtesy if you caught a ride to always offer gas money to the driver, this was an unspoken code that we respected. There was this one woman who drove us all crazy. I would go to her house to pick her up and she was never ready. When we pulled up to her house, she would just be getting home after a night on the town and would ask us to wait outside while she got ready. On top of that, she would get in the car without an apology and ask us to go by the store so she could pick something up to eat for lunch during her shift. Mind you, we were already running late but when I stopped by the store, she had the nerve to take her time finding whatever it was she needed. When I started riding with her, there were four women riding together. Before I knew it, everyone stopped riding in my carpool. The other women could not take her attitude and her making us late. I tried to make it work, so I ended up wearing my clean clothes down with me underground, instead of changing up top first. We rode together for about six months, and I was miserable the entire time.

Another time, I carpooled with a male coal miner. He was a good friend and lived near me. I knew him for at least two years before we rode together. During this time, it was getting cold in Indiana, as it normally does every winter. I remember the temperature was 20 degrees outside with snow on the ground. You did not want to be sitting outside in that cold too long. This obviously did not occur to my friend, who was having an affair with one of the girls at the coal mine. Either that or he just did not care. When he drove, he would make a pit stop by his girlfriend's house sometimes. Now we always met up 30 minutes early. He believed in being on time, so that was never the issue. The problem was, I knew his wife and two daughters well and liked them. He never asked if I cared. Why would a Dog ask about his ways? He would make a stop and say, "I'll be right back." At first, I was clueless as to what was going on. It wasn't until after the second time we stopped that he told me who lived there, and I started to connect the dots. I knew the girl who lived there; she worked at the mine as well but on a different shift. Her boyfriend also worked at the mine on our shift. I knew her boyfriend. I knew his wife and kids and now I must keep the secret, too? The whole thing was a mess. I went off on him for leaving me in the cold car while he was inside getting his rocks off.

After all the shenanigans, I decided I would ride by myself. This one night was a particularly bad night and I couldn't wait until my shift was over so that I could shower and leave. Before I could do that, the mine manager asked a bunch of us if anyone wanted to work overtime. I was the first to speak up. "Nope, I'm going home! See you all tomorrow." I got away from there quickly. I jumped in my car and got off the property as fast as I could. I was so glad that I didn't have to ride with anyone. I was going solo, and everything would be all good. I thought that was what I needed. I was wrong. I needed someone to keep me awake. I had to stop for a train to go by. There were so many cars in front of me that I decided to turn my car off. I was so tired that I fell asleep. When I woke up, the cars behind me were going around me. The cars in front of me were gone. I'm sure that they were honking their horns, but I never heard them. I was asleep for 20 minutes. No one thought to stop to see if maybe I had a heart attack. I was really embarrassed and hoped that no one knew it was me. I waited until the last car passed me to move. After that night, I decided to stay with my adulterous carpool partner.

CHANGES UP AHEAD

I was driving myself to work in blizzard-like weather. It had been snowing all day and the snow was sticking. It was taking forever to get to work. There was so much snow and all I could see was snow around me and on the top of the cars that I was passing. There was just one lane, and I didn't see the sign that said the road was closed. I could barely see outside of my windshield. I drove very slowly trying to get to work. There was a car behind me riding my bumper. I couldn't believe how close they were. All I could see was the lights. I didn't know if it was a small car, truck, or a big semi. I couldn't turn off because the snow covered the embankments. I was a nervous wreck. I knew one thing; I was feeling anxious between the weather and this vehicle riding my tail.

When I got to work, my friend Bill told me he wanted to choke me. He was the one riding my tail and he complained that I was driving too slowly. The lamp man came around and told us the mine was shut down for the night since the roads were closed. He made us sign in and we were paid for four hours of work for showing up. I was livid because I could have stayed home with my kids and gotten some much-needed rest. Instead, I had to make a bed in the women's shower room. It was freezing and to make matters worse, I didn't have a blanket. I slept on a cold bench. I was the only female who drove into work that night. I was supposed to call the highway patrol to see about road closures. After that happened, I had a girlfriend who promised to call me and tell me if the roads were going to be closed. That was the first and last time that happened.

After years of working in the mines, we finally got our first female boss. She knew her job and we trusted her. A modern woman in a man's underworld and she is the boss! Most of the women were excited because we finally thought we had someone who was down with us. How could she not be down with us, way down here? Little did we know our new leader had two faces. One minute she would be cool and the next she would snap and yell, demanding we listen to her because she was the boss. Then, the next day she would bring us food. I told the guys I would not eat her food; she might have poisoned it. They laughed and ate her food; I didn't touch it. I wasn't taking any chances. She would make me a nervous wreck with all that screaming and yelling. She was a big headache. Maybe she was new to the position and felt she had to prove herself but make hard boundaries. Maybe this shrewd anger is how she climbed the ranks. Maybe her meanness made her a proper overseer in her eyes. I wanted to get away from her as soon as possible. She watched over us closely like a hawk. We all got the sense that she didn't fully trust us. My coworkers and I didn't understand what the problem was. I tried to give her the benefit of the doubt; I thought maybe she was going through menopause. We all knew she could be friendly, but she could turn her head and start screaming and shouting at all of us at the drop of a dime. I was disappointed: We had finally got our first female representation of a boss and almost everyone hated her. Maybe it was a lack of maturity or the stress of being a female boss trying to fit in with the other male bosses. When she came, us ladies were overjoyed until she came with the overkill.

One night, one of the guys from my unit was out drinking and he saw our boss at the local bar. She was drunk and flirting with him. They both were single at the time so it could have gone down, but because she was so angry at work, he passed on it and went home. He told us about it the next day. We gave him a tough time and told him he should have taken one for the team. From that point on, she would belittle him in front of everyone and we all suffered from her controlling ways. Thank God I was moved to another unit shortly after.

GOOD NEWS

I was thirty-five, still working on third shift, feeling like a walking zombie. I was tired and the night shift seemed so long. My oldest son, Adrian, was eighteen and had been living on his own with friends for a while. One day he came to my home and said I was going to be a grandmother. I heard him but I didn't. I was in a mental funk from work and so burnt out from daily things at home. My marriage was a struggle, at this point John and I had been arguing and fighting a lot due to his drinking and he would become more physically violent. My two younger children were in school and old enough to get themselves up and out the door in the morning and everything was routine.

The thought of having a grandbaby was exciting. I couldn't wait to go shopping and pick out little baby clothes when I found out I was having a granddaughter. I really liked the young lady my son was having a baby with; she was from Evansville, and I met her the year prior when Adrian went to her prom.

I didn't realize my life would be changed forever. When I first saw her at the hospital, Brittnie filled my heart with so much joy! My love for her was so strong, I snapped right out of my little life funk. Brittnie was beautiful and looked so much like my son. I was immediately smitten with her adorable, gentle, little spirit. Oh, I really loved the role of being a grandmother!

The thought of this bundle of joy, coming from my son and sharing my bloodline was incredible. I would look at her and see my newborn son all over again, but this time I had money and had managed to keep my children alive and well. I didn't have the same insecurities that I once had as a struggling single mom. I was confident and full of joy and love. I would get to watch Brittnie on the weekends from time to time. Being a grandmother was easier than being a mom. It was less stressful; I could spoil my grandbaby as much as I wanted to and return her back to her parents. Suddenly, I had this extra energy; my grandbaby had given me life. When she came around, I was never tired, I wanted to stay up and play with her, take her to the park, and show her off to friends and family. I was needed in an entirely different way, and it was amazing. Brittnie brought so much love into our home, the kids were excited and loved to help when needed, even John was moved by her precious smile.

I enjoyed seeing my son as a dad. I knew he would be a good one because he used to watch over his siblings when I was at work. I could feel his pride when he looked at his daughter, his eyes beamed with joy. He was growing into a man right before my eyes, he was working and found a place for him and his family to live in.

NOT MY TIME TO GO YET

Time, what is time, really? As I continued to work in the mine, my children continued to grow and before I knew it, were all nearly adults themselves. By the time my daughter was in high school, I was back to working the third shift and feeling the effects on my body, my sleep pattern, and my overall wellbeing. After getting off one morning, feeling completely exhausted and depleted, I scrounged up what little energy I had to go pick up Myca from Ball State College. She was attending an Upward Bound weeklong residential program. My play daughter, Sheena, asked me if she could ride with me to pick her up, a request I immediately said yes to. I was glad that she was going with me and knew that having her in the car would help keep me alert on the road. We had stopped for something to eat and when I jumped back on the freeway, I went the wrong way and we got lost. That wrong turn cost us quite a bit of time and I was late picking up my daughter. All the students had to be packed, out of the dorms, and picked up by 6 p.m. When we got there, she was sitting outside with her bags with one of the chaperones.

I was beyond exhausted. The drive home was only 3½ hours and I knew I wouldn't make it the whole way. I drove for an hour and half, then had Myca take over. Myca was a good highway driver, so I felt confident that she would be able to get us home with no problems. I had to be at work the next day, so with Myca driving, I would be able to get some sleep in the back seat. I closed my eyes and drifted off into a deep sleep. The last thing I remember was Myca and Sheena talking. I woke up briefly just in time for Myca to tell me that we were in Patoka, which was about 10 miles from our home. I went right back to sleep.

What I didn't realize was that Myca was tired, too. She was up late every night hanging out with the girls from her dorm. She fell asleep at the wheel and before I knew it, the Jimmy Blazer had flipped several times, and we ended up hitting a corn bin. I was sleeping in the back without a seat belt on and with the impact, I was thrown out of the side window and knocked out. When I came back to consciousness, I could hear Myca screaming because she couldn't find me. The girls both had seat belts on and were blessed to come out without any injuries. I could hear them crying and yelling my name, but I couldn't see. The girls climbed out of the back of the Blazer. I heard Myca say that they had to find me and get out before the blazer caught fire. I knew it was bad because when she found me, she was freaking out. My eye was bulging out of my socket, and I couldn't see out of my left eye. For a second, I thought I had gone blind. All I could hear in that moment was the girls screaming and crying and my daughter repeatedly saying, "Mom I'm sorry. I'm so sorry!" All I could think about was my job. I mumbled to her "to reach for my purse and get my phone". I had Myca call my job and explain what happened. Work was all I knew. Here I was laid out on the side of the road close to death, and I was fearful of getting fired because I had used up all my sick days. Myca then called John, her stepdad, and an ambulance to tell them where we were. A man saw us off on the side of the road and stopped to help us as the ambulance drove right past us. The man called the ambulance again to tell them where we were. They came back and rushed me to the hospital. My vision returned later that evening, but I had suffered a broken back. I was told that I needed to wear a back brace for several months.

John was so angry about the car being totaled and he was a real jerk to me at the hospital. He wouldn't speak to me or even remove the glass shards off my face. He told me to have my daughter take care of me since she was the one who got me in this situation. And take care of me she did. Myca made sure the nurses and doctors were on it and taking care of me. I was devastated by his treatment, and he was getting on my nerves. Cold, callous, and unloving. He was also angry that I could not go back to work. My brother, Bruce, came from Omaha to help me and my family out. Of course, John took issue with this as well and was not happy that my brother was there. Even while bedridden, John wasn't willing to cook, do laundry or take care of the kids; so, he eventually had to get over it. Bruce did not go back to Omaha until I was walking and able to take care of my family and for that, he will always be my heart. The company finally told me that I could come back to work as long as I had my back brace on. They put me on light duty, but I could not clean outside. I was happy to come back to work and I agreed to the restrictions.

After six weeks, I was feeling like my old self again and started cleaning outside. The next thing I knew my boss was standing over me screaming, "I told you not to do this! If I see you doing this again, you will be fired!" He was livid, but I knew he was right. I had to wear that back brace for six months and I hated it. I always had to wear it, except when I was sleeping or in the shower. My back has been broken twice in my life. Once underground and once in a car accident. I remember when my back was so bad that I had to grab on to the walls to get out of bed. I would have constant back spasms. About a year after the accident, my church did a 30-day fast that I participated in. And after 30 days, I received my blessing: I did not need to have back surgery. My life could've ended the moment I was thrown from that blazer, but it didn't. I have had so many miracles and blessings in my life, and even with everything, I know that God isn't done with me yet.

FINDING OUT THE HARD WAY

I wish I would have paid more attention to my grandmother when choosing my second husband, John. My grandmother warned me about men and how to tell the difference between a good man and one who would love me and my children unconditionally and one who wouldn't. My second marriage to John lasted a little longer than my first; we stayed together for almost 14 years. I married a man who was ready for me but was not ready to be a father to the two other children I had previously. He had a steady career. He worked for "Snap It Up" in Mount Carmel, Illinois, for 28 years. Our marriage was sustained and supported mostly from a financial vantage. I was a hard worker who made a great income, and he had a home and stability. I know we loved each other in our own way, and we did well over the years. We had a beautiful home, hosted lots of parties, and always looked like we had it together. Looks can be deceiving.

Financially, we were making over $100,000 a year. I made more at my job, but John worked on cars on the side and always had extra money coming in. We owned nice cars, built additions to our home, pole barns, and lots of material things including 7 lots of land.

At some point, I started to believe our marriage was all about the stability of material things. I wanted a father for my children and a man who would keep a job. John had a dream of what he wanted his castle to be, and I was the perfect partner to give him those things financially. We took love out of the scenario and instead we both became workaholics. Our relationship felt more like a business arrangement than an actual partnership based on love. We kept the illusion of a perfect home up and from the outside looking in, we had it all together. We had a picture-perfect lifestyle, but if you looked closely, you could see the clear and obvious shortcomings. We were dealing with abuse, alcoholism, adultery, and manipulation. But practice leads to perfection in some parts of life, and we were getting a lot of practice.

Our marriage would get so volatile that it became challenging for me to hide or deny what was going on behind closed doors. There were many times that I would go to work with a busted lip or black eye. On occasion, I would go to work with both. I was so embarrassed and thankfully, I worked with a group of understanding people. I knew I probably got on their nerves with my crying all the time. I was no longer able to conceal or hold in the real. I knew who would listen and who wouldn't. Most of the time I didn't say anything at all. It got so bad at home at one point that when I called the police, they made me, and my babies leave. We stayed at the Albany Women's Shelter in Evansville. This was a problem because the shelter was an hour in the opposite direction from the mine. I couldn't tell anyone where we were staying so I would drive back and forth by myself. I made some friends quickly and I had an older woman watching over the kids at night while I worked third shift. Luckily, this was in the summer and the kids were out of school.

The shelter was sad but full of strong women. They were just like me: They were mothers who were being abused and trying to find their next move. I had chores to do in the shelter to keep our room every day. Once I came in from work, my chores were posted on the door waiting for me. The shelter had a nightly curfew that they amended for me so that I could work.

We had some young girls who would miss curfew and get locked out. I was grateful to have somewhere to go with my babies. It was clean and since the women made food, it was always home cooked and decent. I was one of the only women who worked full time. I honestly used my job as my strength. I didn't have time to be sad or even mad. I was too tired. I wanted out of that shelter so badly and wanted to get back into my comfy home. We stayed there for almost a month. We had to wait until the court allowed me to come back because John and I were legally separated. We ended up divorced, bitter, and financially stricken. In our case, it was better to end things than to scar our children any further with the damage of two broken people who had lost the fight.

IT HURT SO BAD

It was pretty much a requirement to have a good pair of sturdy, well-fitted gloves while working the roof belting machine. I saw tough men run the machine without wearing gloves with no problem at all, but not this old girl. I never said that I was tough, and I had no desire to rough up my hands. I needed my gloves. The problem was, I had my old pair of gloves, and they were too big for me, and I had to start my shift. I had purchased a new pair of gloves, but I forgot to put them in my bag that day when preparing to go down. When we got to our unit, I thought that we was going to have a good night since we did not have too much to do. We had to replace old bolts with new ones, which was always an easy job.

We were bolting about two hours into the shift when things took a turn for the worst. It happened so suddenly. My big old gloves wrapped around the steel that drives the hole into the top, pulling and fastening my fingers tightly around it. I screamed the shrillest scream ever. I could not get my finger unwrapped from the steel and the pain was unbearable. The machine was so loud, and I was trying to get my partner's attention. He did not realize what had happened because he was busy putting replacement bolters on his side. We were working on opposite sides of the bolter. Once he realized there was an emergency, he immediately came over and tried to help me get my fingers loose. My attempts to get my fingers free from the turning steel failed. Every time my partner tried to pull my fingers out, I screamed louder. This forced him to stop.

"I told you I have to get your fingers out," he said calmly but firmly. "Quit screaming."

"I know," I replied grimacing. I understood my screaming prevented him from doing what he needed to do. I managed to keep my mouth shut while he peeled and pulled my fingers away from the machine. This was the most agonizing pain I had ever felt. My fingers felt like they were on fire and all my blood rushed to my fingertips.

After he helped release my fingers, I pulled my gloves off and saw that my bone was sticking out of my skin. They kept telling me not to look at it as we traveled back to the top, but I couldn't help it. When we finally got there, I sat in one of the offices, waiting for the ambulance.

"Looks like you will be off for a couple of months," the safety manager remarked after taking one look at my finger. I immediately started crying again. This startled him. It wasn't just the pain but rather the stacking serious injuries on various parts of my body and the mental scars that caused this round of tears.

"Well maybe not but just don't look at it," he said, deciding to revise his statement.

At that time, I was the only one at my house working. I had just gotten a divorce from John, and it was hard being head of the household. My money was the only money coming in and the injury could not have come at a worse time. His words gave me some peace of mind, so I stopped crying and started to think positively. It was not the end of the world because I would be back in a few weeks. After all, it was only a broken finger. I mean, it's not like I lost a finger.

The ambulance finally arrived and took me to Gibson General Hospital in Princeton, Indiana, which was close to where I lived. When the doctor came in to see me, he said I could not eat anything because he was sending me to Evansville for surgery. Since Adrian lived in Evansville at the time, I called him and let him know what happened and where I was at. He and his new wife immediately came to the hospital. They were in the room when the doctor arrived. The doctor assessed my hand and thankfully, he told me that I would not need surgery. I was so glad he said that it automatically meant less recovery time, a quick return to work, and the ability to eat right away. I was of course a workaholic, first and hungry, second. He informed me that it would be as simple as correcting the placement of the bone. It was quick. He told me to look away and just as I did, he firmly took my hand and put the bone back in place. It hurt, but if I did not need to have surgery and I could eat, I would be happy. He then told me that I would be in rehabilitation for about three months. I wanted to start crying all over again.

While in recovery I stayed at my son's home with him and his wife. I had physical therapy three times a week in Evansville. I was required to go for follow-up appointments over the following weeks and when I saw the doctor the first week, I let him know that my index finger was hurting. It turned out that it was broken too. I chose to look at it as a blessing that my fingers were broken and not lost.

During this time Adrian had three additional children, Devon, Aeriana and Tierra. My grandbabies were young, between the ages of 5 and 7 years old. They would see all the bandages on my hands and say to me, "Grandma has an ouchy." I would often take Aeriana with me to therapy sometimes. She was very well behaved during those visits and was so curious about everything. She would tell the doctor, "Don't make my grandma hurt or be in pain." At the same time, when I got home, they would want me to hold them and jump up in my lap because they were their happiest sitting up under me it seemed. They had no idea that using my hands was so painful, but how could a grandmother deny her beautiful granddaughters?

No matter how much I attempted to keep my hands out of harm's way, somehow those precious littles ones would run right into them, and boy did it hurt. I knew that they were little and didn't mean to, but I wanted to scream, nonetheless. They would always ask to kiss my bandages to make it feel better and would say they were sorry, but my fingers would be aching. All I could say was no and ask that they please stay away from my fingers. They were bundles of joy and I felt so loved by them. Now that they are older, they have no time for me anymore. This tickles me because they have grown into lovely young women, with beautiful children of their own.

My hands and fingers have continued to take a beating over the years. I broke my other two fingers on my other hand years later. I was cleaning the top of my roof bolter and as soon as I put my hand on the canopy the top started to fall. All the rock came down fast right after it. I got my hand smashed once again. I made sure that the therapist was right there in Princeton where I lived so I did not need to stay with my son, and I was not off work that long. In short, both of my hands have been messed up, one way or another.

I remember coming out of surgery, waiting in the recovery room when the Doctor announced, "Your finger's not straight." He then proceeded to take my finger and attempt to force it to bend straight. I screamed so loudly he halted his effort. My daughter was with me at the time and asked him firmly, "Why did you do that?" He knew better than to respond. He also told me I would be off work for about four months and wrote a prescription for the pain.

For months, I would wake up from my sleep because of my throbbing fingers. Although it took some time to heal, my fingers no longer give me any issues and I am grateful to have the use of both hands. I'm even more grateful that I didn't develop arthritis. My finger is still bent to this day a small cosmetic flaw but it's a small thing when compared to how much more serious things could have been.

GETTING LAID OFF

When working underground, you would always hear rumors of what's going on behind the scenes on the business side of the company. For many years, there was a rumor that Illinois Coal would shut down, it was circulating for years but because it never happened, none of us really believed it. That changed in what seemed like an instant. I arrived at work one day, and noticed men dressed in street clothes with hardhats going underground. These men would find us while we were working and interview us regarding how Illinois Coal was treating their employees and what we would do if the mine closed. We knew there was a company interested in buying it. The managers never disclosed it, but the rumors were floating all over. We found out later that the mine had hired consultants to come in and spy on us, when in essence we should have been the ones spying on them!

Two weeks later, we had a shift meeting before we went underground and that's when we found out that the mine was closing. The consultants did most of the talking. They told us they didn't know how long the mine would be closed. I was shocked and angry when I was laid off even though I needed the break more than I would ever admit. The first month I slept, did housework, and spent time with my grandchildren. At first, I didn't know what to do with myself or my free time. I was lost. The mine approved us for unemployment, so I was maintaining my bills. They also offered to send us back to school to get G.E.D's or take college classes from a trade program and they promised to pay for it fully. The mine connected us to a Career Center in Evansville. I gained computer, interviewing, and communication skills while there and earned several certificates. I always loved cooking, so I decided to take a food and safety class at Wishbone College. I wanted to start a vendor's booth or food truck.

The class was full of young and energetic 18 to 20-year-old students. I attended night class a couple days out of the week and was the oldest person there. I was even older than the professor. I took a tape recorder to record the classes. I was overwhelmed and on top of all that, the class was long and boring. I made it through three weeks before my first test was scheduled. I dropped the class before the test because I was afraid, I would bomb the exam.

I didn't feel like the continuing education courses were really for me after a while, so I chose to apply at a non-union mine to support and keep my household afloat. I caught some flak for that choice and some of my fellow union brothers and sisters frowned on my decision. I did not have the luxury to care what others were saying about me. I had to put food on my table. What was I supposed to do? Not work, leave my bills unpaid, and let my children starve? No, I had to feed my family and take care of business.

I later got hired at a strip mine in Wholewheat, Indiana. I worked a swing shift, which I despised. I never knew which shift I would be working because it changed each week. I never wrote down my schedule and one day I paid for that big time. I was staying at a friend's home, and I thought that I was supposed to be on day shift. I got to the mine ready to go and one of the guys asked me if I was working over and I told him I was there to start my shift. He informed me that I was scheduled for the second shift that day. I went to the mine manager and asked him if I could work both shifts. He said that it would be Ok. I did not want to do it, but I didn't want to go all the way back home. I worked 16 hours roof bolting that day all because I forgot to write down my schedule.

I THOUGHT I WAS HAVING A HEART ATTACK

I was coughing non-stop and did not feel good at all. It was the middle of November and I felt like my chest was going to cave in. I was on the phone talking with my daughter, who was at college in Las Vegas, and I could barely breathe.

"Hey mom, how are things going?"

"I was going to ask you the same thing," I said while coughing uncontrollably.

I could not hold a conversation with her.

"Mom, you need to get yourself to the doctor, you could be really sick, do I need to come out there?"

"You just worry too much about me, don't come out here," I said, still coughing. I coughed so much that my eyes burned and teared up. The coughing was so painful that I had to get off the phone with her.

I went to the company doctor prior to speaking with my daughter. The doctor sent me home with $97 dollars' worth of medicine and when I asked her for an x-ray, she told me that my lungs sounded fine. "Try and let the medicine work," the doctor said. I could barely breathe or speak without coughing, and she sent me back to work. She declined to look at my lungs, it very well could have been Black Lung. I took the medicine, and I stubbornly went back to work that evening. I was so angry that she sent me back underground, but what did I expect from the company doctor? She only had their best interest in mind, not mine.

I didn't get any better. My chest and back were hurting, and my heart was racing. I thought that I was having a heart attack. My shift was almost over when I found my boss, he told me to stay in the dinner hole until my shift was over. My stomach hurt, I was freezing with body chills, and I could barely breathe. I was so sick that I could not do anything else. I asked the Lord for help and promised that I would go to the hospital. It was another desperate compromise; I was afraid for my life. I tried my best to get out of the mine and to the hospital. I walked up slowly to my car and grabbed on to every rail for support. I could barely balance the weight of my own body. I needed to shower, but I was freezing. My body was sore and achy. It was a battle getting to the freeway. There were construction workers holding up traffic at almost every stop. I thought that I would never get to the hospital. I was afraid that I was going to pass out while driving. Every part of my body hurt as I grabbed the wheel, pressed the brakes, and coughed uncontrollably. I decided to go to the hospital in Vincennes, which was 20 minutes from home. When I finally got to the E.R. they could tell from my gasping for air that I was in bad shape. It was around 4 p.m. and everything felt like it was in slow motion, but they took me back immediately. I was relieved when I recognized a familiar face, a young doctor who had worked in my family doctor's office. He had quit private practice and had become an E.R. doctor at Good Samaritan Hospital. I finally was able to take a deep breath; I knew I was in good hands. Knowledge of care can bring peace in the chaos.

"It's good to see you, Janice," he said, raising his eyebrows. "What are you in here for today?" He asked me this as if he did not already have my chart in his hand. "It is really good to see you too," I said. He ran tests on my chest and came back to give me the results.

"The test shows that you have double pneumonia," he said, then paused. "That means it is in both lungs."

"I knew I did not feel good but..." I said before he interjected.

"You did not feel good because both your lungs are not working," he said curtly, understanding my penchant for ignoring my health and putting my job above all else. They gave me a breathing treatment and he showed me my x-rays.

"What does that mean doctor?" I asked. He knew what I meant.

"It means you need to stay in the hospital for a few days," he said.

"No!" I said. "I have to go to work tomorrow." I knew I needed the days off to rest, but I wanted to be at home. I hated hospitals. They were always freezing cold, and my body had the chills, which went straight to my nerves. I was miserable.

"You must stay in the hospital for a few days," he repeated. "I am going to get a specialist to see you. This specialist is a friend of mine. He will see you tomorrow. You will just be here for two days." He was lying and he probably saved my life doing so. I still trusted him.

I was a sick woman, but I would have got up and gone back to work again. The next day while I was in the hospital, I tried to give myself a bath. I felt so bad that I had to call a nurse, because I could not make it to the bathroom. Instead, she brought me a wash basin so that I could give myself a bath. When I started to wash myself, I could not breathe at all. It scared me so much that I panicked. I began flailing my arms around, similar to the funky chicken. "I can't breathe, I can't breathe," I yelled. The nurse ran out to get help. They needed to give me oxygen, but the nurses needed me to calm down first. Before I knew it, I had three nurses working with me.

"Stay calm Janice," one nurse said.

"Calm down, please. We are here to help you," another nurse chimed in. I was not getting it. I was having a bad feeling.

"We want to give you oxygen," another nurse said. Finally, I started to listen to the nurses. They were trying to get the oxygen tubes to my nose. I let them.

Adrian still lived in Evansville during this time, which was an hour away from the hospital. I had been there at least four days before he called. He showed up later that evening with a friend. I was annoyed that he brought someone with him. I looked rough; I barely had the energy to speak let alone have some non-family member looking at me crazy. He stayed about an hour because they were taking me to get treatments. He must have been really scared. He didn't say much to me, he just stared at me with his sad eyes and worried face. He called his sister and told her that my condition was serious...She needed to come home. A couple days later, Myca walked into my room with a bouquet of flowers and balloons with her brother. I was shocked he didn't tell me that he planned on flying her home. I hadn't heard from my daughter, which was odd, so when I saw her face, I was relieved. My kids did care. I knew I could relax with my daughter there and she would see to it that the nurses were getting my lunch orders, taking me to the bathroom, and changing out my bed linen. I was in the hospital for about two weeks when the Doctor walked into my room:

"When do I get to go home?" I asked.

"You are lucky to be alive. So, don't ask me anymore about going home," he said as if irritated that he cared more about my lungs than I did. I had a lot of doctors coming in and going out of my room. Like busy angels up and down Jacob's ladder. It took a long time for the various medicines to work for me. The first batch of medicines didn't work. Nothing was getting to my lungs. I was in pain and still coughing after the first week when they found the right medicine. They diagnosed me with Chronic Obstructive Pulmonary Disease (COPD). It is a common condition of coal miners. I got it from being in the coal mine for 20 years and from breathing in coal dust. This confirmed that the chewing gum did not help in the least. I thought if I chewed gum that the dust would get stuck in the gum instead of my lungs. I was told that I would have COPD for the rest of my life. It was not going away and there was no cure.

When I got out of the hospital, I went to see the lung specialist at the doctor's office. I really liked him. He put me on not one, not two but three different types of inhalers for the COPD and he gave me a shot for the pneumonia.

"You must be a smoker," the nurse said as she was giving me the prescription.

"No, I am a coal miner," I said, correcting her.

"Oh yes, that would make sense," she said, not even missing a beat or showing any empathy for her assumption.

When I got out of the hospital, I told my doctor I had to go back to work. He insisted that I needed time to heal.

"Take some time off," he said. I disagreed with him. He sent me back to work three days later and I did not make it the whole day. I got to work and before I could get out of the cage, I was gasping for air. I couldn't breathe. I started to feel dizzy and lightheaded. I left work and drove straight to my lung specialist. I had a relapse and had to go back to the hospital. This time I stayed a full week. I had only myself to blame. Just like the thigh leg cast for my ankle that I tested, I had to try my way. Again, the mine was the reason behind my physical ailments; almost all.

"You have a hard head," my doctor told me, visibly perturbed.

"I know that" I said. He was so mad at me, but I blamed the company doctor.

When I finally went home, I found out that my sons had a good old time in my absence. My house was so dirty. My bed had been slept in. It was as if Brownie Locs had come into my home and tried everything for size. I was infuriated to the point where I was thinking about having them give me their copies of the house keys. I was not able to clean or even change my bed linen, so I slept in my reclining chair until I felt better. I must have slept in that chair for a week. My daughter had gone back to school, and I was alone. My sons were in and out, but they didn't understand that I needed someone to care for me or at least bring me some chicken noodle soup. Some of my things were even missing. This was very upsetting but in the grand scheme, I just did not care anymore. I was alive and that was all that mattered. Although I was still mad at my sons, I needed to focus on getting better.

I had to look at the brighter side of things. Even though I had COPD, a lot of my friends carried oxygen tanks around and I did not. I could walk around freely whereas many others with COPD could not. My biggest challenge was remembering to take the medicine. It took six months before I felt like I could breathe normally again. That was one of the hardest things that I have ever experienced. I had to literally fight for every breath.

ONLY THE STRONG SURVIVE

N ot everyone was happy that I worked in the mines. Racism was alive and present in the early 80s and I experienced it at all three mines I worked for. Don't forget I was still living in Southern Indiana, north klan central. I'll never forget the first time I saw it with my own eyes. I was riding through a unit at Illinois Coal and when I looked up, I saw kkk painted in red with the Swastika symbol next to it. No one on the unit uttered a word. I was taken aback and shocked. It never occurred to me that I worked with people who belonged to a hate group. I lived in Southern Indiana and had previously heard of incidents with the kkk before, but never experienced it firsthand. There were hoods around me, and I did not think to see; I was just happy to work. They wanted to be seen. They wanted me to know I was black in a white man's mine. I had family members who had crosses burned in their front yard. As a black woman, it was scary.

It didn't stop there though. About two years later there was a black man hired as a unit boss. He was the first black manager the mine ever had. Not even a couple weeks into his time at the mine, he was harassed. He would come to work and find nooses hanging in his unit and he was often followed home after work. Terrifying and tactics of intimidation, an escalation of stalking one's prey. A portrayal of plausible violence. He ended up quitting. Around the same time, I remember walking to my unit and seeing a noose hanging from the roof bolt. There were at least eight men standing around the dinner hole and no one seemed to notice the dangling rope. I walked right past it with my head held high. I refused to give them the satisfaction of seeing me scared. If they wanted to play ignorant to the noose, then so shall I. So, with my head high, I made my money.

There was only one time where I thought my life was in real danger. There was a group of men on the two-way radio discussing all the details for the klan's meeting. My heart sank. I heard someone say, "You know she can hear you." A guy spoke up and said, "I don't care if she can." I was terrified. I had a friend who later told me that the conversation I overheard was about a real kkk meeting but told me not to worry because the bosses had overheard the guys talking and had reprimanded them and promised that it wouldn't happen again. In some way, the snakes will reveal themselves again. I left so quickly that day, I didn't even shower. I was at that mine for over three years and from that point on, I never let my guard down. I knew they didn't want me there. Some men felt that I only got my job due to affirmative action. There was one individual who got in my face once and screamed at me that I took a job away from his friend, who in his opinion was a qualified white man. I was shocked and told him that if he had a problem, he needed to talk to the Mine Rep. I also told him I never lied on my application that I wasn't a man so how could I have taken a man's job away. He left that day and I never saw him again. Looking back, I was mentally stronger than I gave myself credit for. Also, more spiritually dense, and grounded. In those situations, I was always quiet and kept my mouth shut. I wanted to work, make good money and most importantly, earn my co-workers' respect. I knew even then that the only way to achieve my goal was to learn my job and work hard. As a black woman, I have dealt with racism my whole life, but this was different. I had to learn how to play the game. They would one day become like the grumpy old man at the nursing home, I hoped in time.

TAKE YOUR FOOT OFF THE BRAKE

While working in Wholewheat, for about six months I finally found a team to carpool with. Two other miners, who lived in the same small town, asked if I wanted to start riding with them. I was all about saving money, so I said yes without hesitation. They were nice guys. Both were younger than me and both had wives and children. They seemed to be happy. This was a smaller mine about 200 feet below ground. There were only about five women and of course, I was the only person of color who worked there.

When it was my turn to drive our carpool, I was a nervous wreck. The guys liked to take all the backroads to get to work, claiming it was a shortcut. I hated those dark winding roads. The bumps from the uneven trails and the narrowness of the way. The fear of deer running in front of our truck and getting into another serious accident. The roads were so curvy that I kept my foot on the brake. As I edged up on the turns, the guys would give me a hard time and told me to relax and just drive. I remember the anxiety of the drive got to me so much that I thought about riding alone. It took a month for me to get comfortable driving to work with those two boys. After many nights of them yelling and working with me, I learned how to drive just like them. I was proud. I knew it was a little accomplishment, but it was my little accomplishment and I proved to those knuckleheads that I could do it. I rode with them for six months. Eventually, I had to take some time off, due to me being sick. When I got back, the two guys were no longer riding together. I heard one of them went on to become a boss. He worked a different shift and stayed late to study. The other one rode by himself until I got back to work.

 While I was away, the young man who stayed on the same shift had gotten into a bad accident. He went on to tell me how it happened. One evening while driving home from work, it was very foggy and dark outside. He was going downhill fast and lost control of the car, driving right into somebody's home. The owner was home on the other side of the house, and he missed her by minutes. He was blessed because he barely missed the tree next to the house, which would have surely killed him instantly. His car was destroyed, and he managed to escape without any injuries. When we started riding together again, and when it was my turn to drive, he was adamant about seeing my car insurance paperwork. He was still shaken up badly from that accident. I understood as I too, had new apprehensions while driving. He wanted to ensure that my insurance would cover both of us if we were in an accident. He was also concerned about property damage; he needed to see what it was and how much coverage I had. He was a nervous wreck and immediately apologized for the way he and his friend harassed me prior to the accident. Instead of being a speed racer, he wanted me to drive slowly and cautiously. He even asked me to keep my foot near the brake if that made me more comfortable. Experience brings understanding.

The house he hit was on the way to the mine; we drove past it every day. The house had a giant hole in the center of the frame and nothing else was there but a tree. It looked awful. The house was wrapped in plastic and zoned off. I kept thinking to myself how the hell did the woman survive that. He would look out the window in despair each time, assessing if the work was done or not. He was paranoid because he didn't have enough property damage insurance to cover the house. He knew the owner could sue him and that he was at fault. His whole life changed in one night from his reckless driving. Those boys gave me such a hard time with my driving that I was always on edge. Thank God I kept my cool under pressure. I was trying to fit in with them and yet, I could have been the one to crash us all.

BAD FEET, BAD BOOTS, GOOD DOCTOR

![horizontal rule decoration]

My feet took a serious beating with all the standing I did at work. And as much as I tried different insoles, new boots, extra cushioned socks, nothing could diminish the pressure and pain my feet endured. We had to wear steel-toe boots when I first started to work at the mine. I always had trouble with my feet because of these shoes. I tried different kinds of boots, different brand names over the years and spent a lot of money. They were not cheap, but I was still somehow disappointed. My feet still hurt! It was not athlete's foot, but I felt constant fire on my heels. It got so bad that my feet would be in excruciating pain not even 20 minutes into my shift. I wanted to cry. Every step I took was unbearable. Each time this happened, someone else would tell me to try a different brand and I would take their advice and buy it.

Then the mine officials required us to wear metatarsal boots. They claimed they were not like the steel-toe boots and were supposed to be better. They had a metal piece in them that not only covered the toes but the entire top of the foot. My feet did not like them either; they hurt worse than before. This went on for years. My feet were in bad shape.

One day, I was talking to a co-worker who gave me some sage advice.

"Janice, you should try inner-soles for your feet."

"I already have them in my boots," I told him.

"Not the ones that you buy at a store," he said, genuinely wanting to help. "You have to go to a foot doctor, that way he can make a pair to fit your feet."

I went to several doctors before I found the right one. Once I did, those insoles made all the difference. At the time, I didn't know whether the insoles would work or not and it cost a lot of money. I had to pay $500 for the insoles beforehand, which admittedly made me a little nervous. Once I received them, I put them in my boots and went underground to see if they would work. And thankfully, the insoles worked. And what was even better, my insurance reimbursed me the $500.

My complaints about my feet hurting stopped and I was able to be on my feet with no pain. When you work on your feet all day, you can't afford to have your feet hurting all the time. I wish I had known about podiatrists earlier. Although they were rather expensive, I am so glad I went to them and bought the insoles. My feet were glad I bought them, too. Building relationships with others is what made the difference for me. In this case, just talking to someone and being open to learning things helped me address the pain in my feet. If I never had that conversation, who knows how much longer I would have been in extreme pain. At the rate I was going, I'm sure my feet would have gone on strike against me.

TO PENNSYLVANIA I GO

F ive years had passed since I was laid off from Illinois Coal, and I was ready to get back to working with a union mine, so I could add to my union time to get my full pension. The only problem was that there weren't too many of them around. In fact, the nearest one was in Pennsylvania, which was about 10 hours away. I really thought about going to Pennsylvania to work in their union coal mine when we all got laid off but instead opted to work for the local non-union mines. Most of the miners from my company were interested in the mines in Pennsylvania because they paid well, and we could continue to add to our union hours. My baby sister was in college at the time and wasn't too far from the mine. Which meant I would have some family close by in case I took a job there. My children were all adults, my baby son was living with his father.

To work in any of the Pennsylvania union mines, you had to take a test and pass it before you could be hired into the company. I hated taking tests. I did not like them in school. I would study, but, when it came time to take the test, I would freeze and forget everything I had studied for. This test was written, oral, and the last part was putting together a miner's lamp and describing each part in front of the test instructor. I had a lot of good people helping me to study for the exam, which included a co-worker's wife who I met with three times a week. My daughter and her friend went with me on the trip to Pennsylvania. I drove all the way there while they quizzed me and asked me questions. I was resolved to be confident, prepared and to remember.

By the time we arrived at our hotel in Pennsylvania, my nerves were shot. While we were shopping for food to bring back to our room to cook, I could not stop thinking about the test. I thought about the test so much that I made myself sick. I did all of that worrying for nothing because I took the test the next day and I passed it. It turns out that in my worrying, I had prepared adequately to pass the test with ease. I was so glad it was over, and we could go back home. As fate would have it, I received a call from Illinois Coal two weeks after taking my test, to come back to work in my previous role and I jumped on it. I really didn't want to go to Pennsylvania, but I would have and was prepared to.

I COULDN'T SHUT MY EYES

I t was Valentine's Day and another cold winter night; I had been back at Illinois Coal for three years now. I was scheduled to work my shift with my good friend, Tom, who I worked with from time to time. Tom and I were close. He liked to wear bib overalls every day. He told me that he liked to collect coins and trade them. We laughed and shared funny family stories. I enjoyed talking with Tom because he loved God and was a good husband and father. He adored his wife. He always had a little smile, and his eyes would sometimes light up when he talked about his wife. I teased him about Valentine's Day and asked him what he got his wife. I had to make sure he knew that all women liked gifts. He told me they had a good day. "I can't wait for my daughter's wedding in June," he exclaimed, beaming like a proud father. I remember us talking about the wedding plans and preparations. Tom had told me in previous conversations that he had less than three years left before he could retire. He wanted to go back to Pennsylvania with his family and had it all planned out, another reason I respected him. He seemed to know what he wanted for his family.

Some miners thought Tom was peculiar because he spoke of the Bible frequently. I had no problem with it or anything he talked about. A few years earlier when I was still married to John, he was working on a car at home in the garage and while he was removing a gas tank, his pants caught fire because he had propane on his trousers. He ended up with third degree burns. Tom and his wife came to the hospital, which was 30 minutes away, to support me. I was surprised at how kindhearted they were. They never called, they just showed up. It meant a lot to me, and his wife was a sweetheart. I was tired and stressed out from driving back and forth to the hospital and working late at night. We had been in and out of the hospital for months and Tom and his wife were offering whatever support they could.

Tom and I knew as we started our shift that night that the area, we were working in was dangerous. The examiner warned me earlier that week that the top was squeezing down and it had been that way for a while. The mine manager knew it too, as well as anyone else who worked down there. 'Squeezing down' meant that the ribs holding the wall were sticking out and would poke us as we walked by; they were buckling. This happens because the ribs are weak and as a result, chunks of coal begin to pop out. Eventually, the ceiling falls in, closing the little space we work in, hence the term "squeeze."

I normally did not get the opportunity to work side by side with Tom, but on this night, the machine that he and his partner Peter used was faulty. Our boss decided to send them over to help Jim and I make up bolts. They were to do this while the mechanic repaired their roof bolting machine. Tom usually worked on the opposite side of me and my partner Jim. Tom was a roof bolter as well. While Jim and I were bolting, Tom and Peter were both behind us, handing us glue and bolts. We were a well-oiled team.

We had not been working too long before things fell apart. We had placed two rows in. The roof bolter was coming down the middle. The buckling rib was on my left-hand side, and suddenly the ceiling made a loud weird noise. We all heard it, and I knew something was seriously wrong. It sounded like the loud thundering crack of wood splitting at lightning speed and a simultaneous sound of something shattering, crushing, and grinding in the empty space. It was a noise I had never heard before and never did again. Initially, I was in front of Tom and the last thing I remember was him standing right beside me. We both looked up at the same time. I saw the coal coming down and I took off running. It came down like heavy black hail with a deafening beat. The supported ceiling began to fall in behind us, which was our way out.

I quickly ran around the front of the 15-foot machine under the unsupported side of the ceiling along the ribs on the opposite wall and back towards the end of the machine. They tell you never to go under unsupported roof areas, but my instinct told me otherwise. I ran so fast that I didn't remember passing Jim on the opposite side. Strangely enough he later said that he did not see me pass him either. I say it was nothing but God. I could not tell you how I got to the back of the machine or why Tom was not behind me. It all happened so fast.

"We got two people down, Tom and Janice!" I remember hearing one of my co-workers say.

"I'm not down," I told them. "But we have to get Tom out!" I hollered. I felt so helpless. I could not be still.

"You gotta get him outta there!" I kept screaming.

"We don't think he made it, Janice." Even after they told me they did not believe he made it, I kept repeating that they had to get Tom out of there.

"You gotta get Tom!" I was frantic. "You gotta get him outta there!" I was crying and shouting uncontrollably. Apparently, the coal and rock came down so fast that it covered Tom up immediately. Jim and I waited while they uncovered Tom. It was like a bad dream, and it would not stop. I just wanted to wake up fast. We had a radio and we heard them say that they were bringing Tom out.

"You gotta get her outta here!" one of the guys said. "Take her to the dinner hole." I did not want to go. I wanted to wait until I saw Tom's face again. I walked back to the hole and waited to hear a word. I was praying for Tom. One of the trucks carried Tom's body. As it rolled by me, I saw them doing CPR on Tom while heading out of the mine. I lost it and that's when I realized Tom was possibly never coming back.

I had to wait in the dinner hole until my shift ended before they finally brought me back up top. I kept thinking that if I had not run, I would have been right there next to Tom. I do believe that he was running right behind me, because that is where they found him, right where I began to sprint. The feds arrived at the scene within hours of the tragedy. They interviewed us, two at a time, inside an empty office. The federal agents, coal executives, and coroner circled around us. During questioning, one of the guys harassed me about running under the unsupported top and immediately another agent cut him off and said that's what saved her. I felt then that they wanted to blame us. The questioning was overwhelming. I was trying to process the fact that I just lost a friend, and I almost lost my life. I was tired and emotional; I began to cry uncontrollably. Finally, I was released to go take my shower. On my way to the shower room, I remembered a conversation that took place a week prior.

"Why are you still working here?" a union examiner asked. "Y'all shouldn't even be in here; you can use your individual safety rights, you know, or somebody's gonna get hurt!"

I wanted to tell him that we were all down there because of company greed and personal necessity. If I was not there, someone else would have been and if I protested, I may have lost my job altogether. None of us could afford that. That examiner knew that the mine wanted every bit of coal by any means necessary. Of course, I never said that. And when it would have mattered most, during the hearing, the examiner never testified in court.

The night Tom died, the company called his wife Sheery and told her to meet them at the hospital. They did not even let her know that her husband was dead until after she arrived at the hospital. They then asked her to sign a paper saying that she could not sue them. She could have been set financially for life if she did not sign those papers. The mine knew that we should not have been working on the spot where the accident happened. The union even had proof but somehow none of that protected any of us. They said they would pay her his salary as if he was still alive. They failed to tell her that his salary would stop being paid after his retirement, which was only three years later. Unfortunately, she did sign the paper without knowing what she was really signing and later regretted doing it. They took advantage of her.

Sherry consulted an attorney afterwards and discovered that there was nothing a lawyer could do. I still feel sick about it. I know that was not what Tom would have wanted for his family. Tom had also told Sherry that he was worried about the area he was working in. Everyone knew about the squeezing. None of us had any business working in that area, but we were scheduled there anyhow. Much later, Sherry shared with me that prior to the tragedy, Tom had begun to use up all his vacation time. She said he had told her that he sensed something bad was about to happen. He even warned his wife that if the mine ever called her and informed her that he was in the hospital, that he would be dead. This broke my heart. His violent end, the wonderful family he left behind, the idea that he knew he was going to die, and the fact that the mine wanted to wash their hands of any liability, was all so sad. That was all he was to them, a loss they wanted to write off.

Tom's death changed me. I realized I was just a number to them, and my life became more valuable to me. Coal mining at that time was a big business but how they handled Tom's death was all wrong, they were able to cover themselves and walk away. My co-workers and I were never the same after that night. I could not even imagine what Tom's family was going through. He was supposed to enjoy his life and walk his daughter down the aisle. He only had a couple years left before he would have received his 30-year retirement package with full benefits. He had a big heart, he was well liked, and is missed by his family and friends.

The coal mine administrators said that they would excuse anyone who wanted to go to Tom's funeral. Everyone expected the mine to be closed that morning so we could all attend; however, they only excused the unit that worked with Tom on the night of the accident, which meant you had to use an unexcused personal day. Everyone was upset. We all went, out of respect; he was so loved and respected. The church was packed with all the coal miners, his family, and his brothers and sisters in Christ. This tragedy impacted me greatly and I realized something I probably always knew but was never faced with up-close: I could die any day. Corporate considered us little people and it was clear in their actions that our safety and wellbeing was not their priority.

After that tragic Valentine's Day, I did not want to be a miner anymore. Although I worked two more years after the accident, I was not the same. I was a nervous wreck. I would jump whenever I heard any noise. Every underground shift, I was on edge and if I heard something start to grind or groan, I wanted to run. I was no longer fearless or as strong-willed as I once was. Everything scared me. I even broke down on the stand in court.

I know that life goes on, but I could not move. After all the injuries and broken bones, I had to get out. I began to constantly think about what was going to happen to me. I began telling many of my co-workers that I was leaving as soon as I got my 20 years in. I knew that I had two more years to go. Before my last year was over, I gave the mine my termination date. At that point, I understood the dangers of the mine from the perspective of a frightened woman who was no longer invincible. I tried to prove that I could stay but it was pointless. I did not care anymore, and I kept thinking that it might be my time to go next. Death can do that to you; it hangs in the air. I could not control my mind anymore, not as much as I used to anyway. Tom's death is something that will be with me for the rest of my life.

One night before our shift, a coworker told me that Tom's son came to the mine inquiring about his father's death. He only had one question: Did my dad suffer? He was an adolescent with questions that very few would have the answer to. He knew that his father did not like pain and was anguished over it.

"Your father did not feel a thing," my co-worker said, reassuring Tom's son.

He was just a teenager when all of this happened. My heart was broken for him and his family. Tom's son probably has a family of his own now, one that Tom will never get to see, all because of corporate greed.

KNOCKED OUT

I was tired and burned out. I remember looking at the coal rib on the side of me. It didn't look good, and I knew something was not right. Just as I was thinking this, the rib came down and knocked me unconscious. When I finally came to, my coworker told me not to move. I was in a lot of pain. All I could think about was how badly I wanted to retire from the mine. I was taken out on a stretcher, but this time it was different. I was scared. After Tom died, I lost the will to be there anymore. I stayed in the hospital overnight and was released the next afternoon. I was bruised all over the right side of my neck, shoulder, and down my back. I could barely walk.

I was assigned to a pain management doctor back in Evansville and had to visit him three times a week to get shots in my neck and back. When the doctor asked me what to put for my return-to-work date, I told him I was done. He thought I was kidding. I had already given the mine my release papers the month after the accident. I knew I would never go back underground. I was done mentally, and my body could not take another beating. It took six months for me to heal from that injury. Even to this day, I still have issues with my shoulder, neck, and back although the pain is bearable.

MR. EARL

I was finally retired, and I didn't have a clue what I was going to do next. I decided to place an ad in the local newspaper about sitting and caring for elderly people. I enjoyed the work, and it made me feel good to take care of people. I got a call from a nice gentleman named Mr. Earl offering me a position to care for his wife, who had been diagnosed with dementia. I went to their home the next evening to meet with them and find out what my daily work would be. I met Helma, his wife, a very tall and thin woman. I could tell she was beautiful in her day. She was quiet but friendly. I found out that she was able to walk and shower on her own.

Mr. Earl was a short and stubby man, who was in his 80s but in good health. He was friendly and easy to get along with. I remember telling him over the phone that I was a black woman, and asking if they would be okay with that, to which he laughed and told me that some of his closest friends from the service were black. He had served in three different wars during his 28 years of service. Mr. Earl and his wife had a dog they rescued from the pound named Buddy who was the love of their life. They didn't have any children, so Buddy was spoiled and well treated. I explained to Mr. Earl that I had recently retired and that this would be a short-term position for me while I waited for my monthly pension to kick in. I knew that I could only accept the position temporarily until it was time for me to move to Vegas. I had about a six to seven-month window. He needed someone immediately who he could trust in his home with his wife, so he agreed.

In the beginning, I started my shift at 8 a.m. and worked until 8 p.m. I did light housework and cooked breakfast, lunch, and dinner. I enjoyed working there. The work was easy, and the pay was great. I was there for less than a month before Mr. Earl asked me to move in. Helma had sundowners and she would roam and get up in the middle of the night. He was scared she would leave and try to drive or walk down the street. I ended up putting a bell on her nightgown so I could hear when she moved. I lived with them and would go home on Sunday morning to check on my stuff. Mr. Earl was sad when I finally had to quit. He offered me an unbelievable cash salary to stay. He was good to me while I worked there. After I left, the two people who worked there took advantage of them by stealing and demanding money and time off. With no true help and no one that he felt he could trust, Mr. Earl ended up putting Helma in a nursing home about a year later.

ON TO VEGAS I GO

I was ready for life after the mine and started getting things in order to move. My brother Bruce came in from Omaha to help me with my cross-country relocation. Out of all my siblings, I was closest to him. Bruce is kind and has a gentle spirit, but I always felt protected around him because he was scrappy and liked to fight if he needed to. Bruce arrived the following month and helped me pack boxes, unload the storage unit, and pack the moving truck. I was so grateful for his help. Adrian showed up with a friend to help but all he did was yell out orders. It took us a week to get everything ready to go. I was excited and nervous all at the same time. It was happening so fast that I didn't have time to worry about anything negative. I spent the last week with my sons, grandkids, and friends and said my goodbyes. My last stop was by little John's house. He had just gotten into a new relationship with an older woman and was excited to tell me he was getting married. He was healthy and in a good place and he seemed happy, which gave me peace. I thought he was too young to get married, but I went with it.

My brother wanted to drive to Omaha to finish some business before we went to Vegas. I was happy about that; it gave me a chance to see my mom and my siblings. It only took us nine hours to make the drive. When we arrived, my mother had a meal prepared for us. After we ate, my mother called the rest of my siblings to tell them we were there. My sister Ruth, my brother Clyde and his wife Tracey, and aunt Ilene all came over. They stayed for a couple hours, leaving me with time alone with my mother, who was sick at the time, but I didn't know it. Mom and I sat in the living room and talked most of the night. My brother arrived at six the next morning so we could start our journey early. We said our goodbyes and we were off. I did most of the driving from Omaha to Colorado, which took us about 11 hours. I enjoyed my brother's company; we talked and laughed a lot and took in the changing landscape around us. He mostly told me stories about when he served in the war, about the streets of Omaha, and shared some family secrets. Overall, the drive was smooth until we got to Colorado. It was only the beginning of March, so the weather was cold and foggy. I was getting tired and didn't realize that I was driving on the shoulder of the highway. My brother woke up and said, "Hey sis, I think you're driving on the wrong side of the road." I told him we would stop to get a hotel room. I was exhausted. I couldn't believe I made it that far. When we checked into the hotel, the manager told us that the night before there was a bad ice storm and that's what caused the fog. The room was clean, and we couldn't wait to take hot showers and go straight to bed. It was so late when we pulled in that I didn't see the mountains that surrounded us. Colorado was beautiful, the air was crisp, and everything smelled so fresh.

The ride to Vegas was smooth. We ran into traffic here and there but overall; the drive went well. When we got into Vegas it was late. My daughter had a two-bedroom apartment near the strip, and it was easy to find. I was so happy to see her and get out of that truck. We spent the next week unloading and unpacking. My brother wanted to see our father while he was there. That following week, Bruce and I caught a Greyhound to Sacramento, California. The ride was long and all I remember was sleeping on the way there. We were still exhausted from the drive across the Midwest. We stayed the weekend with our father, it was the first time either of us had seen him in a long time.

The ride back to Vegas on the Greyhound was crazy; my brother and I didn't get to sit next to each other. My brother made sure to tell me that the bus was filled with inmates who just got released from jail. The first hour was quiet, then all hell broke loose when a fight started out in the back of the bus. My brother was sitting a couple rows behind me. I didn't want to be nosey, but I had to keep looking back to make sure Bruce was Ok. The fight got so bad people started running to the front of the bus. The bus driver called the police and told them to meet us at the next station. As soon as we pulled up, we were all told to get off and the two men who were fighting got arrested. I couldn't wait to get back to Vegas. That was the last time I rode the Greyhound. My brother stayed with us for almost two months before he went back to Omaha.

DANCING INTO A NEW ADVENTURE

Myca couldn't wait to take me out on the town. We would go out dancing almost every night and I loved it. I worked so hard at the coal mine that I rarely got to go out. On the days I was off from the mine, I was so busy raising my kids that I didn't get out much. Vegas was totally new to me. Myca would pick out my clothes and shoes. Sometimes I liked it and most of the time I felt like I was too old to be dressed like a teeny bopper.

Myca had worked in several nightclubs in the city and had made friends all over. She had a different place that we would go to every night of the week that was jumping. We had a Latin club on Thursday that we loved going to. We were often the only black women there, but we didn't care. We thought we could salsa and merengue with the best of them. Sometimes, we would go to the after-hours club and come home when the sun was coming up. I didn't realize how much my daughter liked to drink. In the past when I came to visit, we would go out, but I had no clue how much she really liked to party. I had a blast though. We would dance and laugh and go get breakfast early in the morning. Sometimes we would get dressed up and go out to these fancy dinners. I felt like a new woman. We also went to church on Sundays, then we would head to a restaurant to have lunch where they always played live jazz music. I really enjoyed the crowd because everyone often got out of their seats and joined in the dancing. Sometimes we would just watch and sometimes I would be asked to dance. For those first few months in Vegas, all Myca and I did was party and celebrate my arrival and retirement. The live concerts were amazing. I got to see musicians up close and personal. The lounges in the casino also had incredible live acts.

LOVE AFTER 50

After a few months, I started to look for work. I was getting bored during the day while my daughter was working. I went to a nearby temp agency to complete an application. They told me the only thing they had available was construction work for general labor. I told them I was open to it. The pay was every week on Friday and the work was easy. I was hired about a week later after my background check cleared. My first job from the agency was at a grocery store where we needed to move shelves for a renovation. Once again, I was the only woman working in an all-man crew. This work was so different compared to the work in the mines. I was done with my shift in eight hours, I was clean, and it was near the house. The guys treated me nicely, they worked hard and kept to themselves.

My job changed every couple of days. Different companies who needed extra people would call in and hire our services. The most stressful thing for me at that time was driving around the city to all the new locations. Las Vegas was a big city. I would sometimes get turned around just driving to the grocery store. My daughter knew the city well. She would write down the directions or spend time with me on the phone guiding me to the area. I knew this job would be temporary because my daughter had me fill out an application at the Wynne Hotel, so we were patiently waiting for them to call so I could get hired on full time with benefits, as a security guard. I ended up working construction for about six months before I got the call. My last construction job was at a hospital doing clean-up duty. I put in my two-week notice and told my boss I was leaving to work with my daughter. He was nice and understanding. On my last day at work after my shift was done my boss ran over to my car and tapped on the window and gave me his number, in case I needed any help. I was shocked and surprised.

My daughter was in Florida visiting a girlfriend, so I called her to ask her about my boss and whether she thought he was hitting on me. Immediately she shut me down saying, "No he just gave you his number to be nice, don't call him." Sometimes my daughter treated me like I was her daughter and not her mother. The conversation was short and to the point. I could tell she was busy because we didn't discuss it any further. I, on the other hand, was curious. I worked under my boss, Nate, for several months. He was quiet and we barely interacted. I remember my coworkers introducing themselves to him. He was from New York and recently divorced. He was always professional around me, so it didn't seem like he was interested. I called him the following day, which was a Saturday. We talked for about 20 minutes. He was glad that I called and invited me to hang out with a group of coworkers for drinks and dinner. He offered to pick me up around seven that evening.

Nate is around 5'8, slim to medium build, with dark hair and dark eyes, and of Italian descent. I found him extremely attractive outside of work. Nate was easy to talk to. He asked genuine questions about my past and he wanted to know the things that I was interested in. That night we ended up having dinner alone. The coworkers ended up at another bar. I'm still not sure if he set that up or they really didn't show. Afterwards, we drove to a casino in Henderson to hear live music. We danced for hours and went over to the VIP area. Somehow, Nate talked the security guard into letting us sit on the cabana beds. It was a gorgeous night. We talked even more and snuggled close together and Nate leaned in and kissed me. I immediately felt a close connection to him. I knew we had chemistry.

The lounge was closing, and he dropped me off at home. All I could think about was how much fun we had and how much I enjoyed his company. Nate and I moved quickly. As you get older, you realize life is short and you don't have time for regrets. We started hanging out every day and I eventually moved in with him to help him take care of his dying father. My daughter came home about a month later and was upset about me rushing into a new relationship. I had started my new job at the Wynne and was in a week-long orientation. My daughter would try and schedule her lunch around mine so we could catch up. I would go home on the weekends, grab clothes, and hang out with my daughter. My job consisted of checking employee badges, greeting, helping casino guests, and being the ears and eyes of the casino. I was appreciative of the work. It was clean, safe, and fun. I got to see celebrities like Bow Wow, the late Robin Williams, and Louis Anderson up close and personal. I'm sure I saw athletes as well, but I didn't know their names, or which sports they played. We had so many people coming and going daily.

One time, I accidentally dropped some casino chips on the floor. I walked the chips over and placed them on the table without the cover and all the chips fell on the ground. I scrambled to pick up the chips as fast as I could. None of the guests tried to take them. I thought I was going to get fired later that afternoon. In total, there was $70,000 worth of chips. I was told that if just one chip was missing, I would have lost my job. That was the only time anything crazy like that happened that was my fault. I really liked my boss. He was fair and knew his job well. He treated all of us with respect.

Nate asked me to marry him within the first month of dating. I was excited and immediately said, "Yes." I knew I had to talk with Myca before I could really move forward. I was thinking that we were moving too quickly. I knew I trusted him and loved him, but I had also gone to hell and back with my ex-husband, so I had my concerns. Myca immediately said that we should wait and didn't understand the rush. The following week the three of us met over lunch. Myca expressed her concerns and we agreed that we would wait a year so that she could get to know Nate better.

A year passed by and out of the blue, Nate looked at me and said if we were going to get married that we needed to do it that day. That afternoon, we went to a chapel where Myca and her friend met us and just like that, we were married. Nate continued to work as a supervisor for his company and we eventually moved to California for his job. We spent the next 14 years traveling around California, Oregon, and Arizona because of his job, which granted us plenty of opportunities to see so many places. They also sent us on an all-inclusive vacation to the Bahamas because of Nate's hard work, which we enjoyed. We normally spend two to four years in a city before moving to a new location, which helps keep our relationship fresh and fun. Sometimes on Nate's days off we go for long motorcycle rides along the coast. My mother-in-law moved in with us in 2018 and she and I have become close. When Nate is working, mom and I spend the day together having lunch, running errands, and shopping. I am grateful for her friendship. I love my husband and I am grateful we get along well. I appreciate all the things he has done for me and my family.

My life has had its share of difficult storms. Thankfully, every single test turned out to be my testimony. Working at the coal mine afforded me and my family some wonderful opportunities and taught me how to grow into a woman. I have been blessed to be in good health at my age. Exercise is a lifestyle for me to manage and keep the C.O.P.D. in check. I have lost many of my mining co-workers over the last 10 years due to poor health or chronic injuries that slowly aged and killed them. My body aches constantly from the breaks and surgeries. I have had my nose broken, my back broken twice, my vertebrae in my neck damaged, my ankle run over, and two fingers on each hand broken at different times. But here I am still standing with so much more life to live. You could say I sold my body for a good paycheck, and I wouldn't argue with you. One thing is for sure: I am a stronger woman because of it and there's very little I would change. I thank God for the grace upon my life and for his divine protection during my life's most challenging times.

www.ingramcontent.com/pod-product-compliance
Lightning Source LLC
LaVergne TN
LVHW051243080426
835513LV00016B/1716